THE ATHLETIC EQUESTRIAN

THE

ATHLETIC EQUESTRIAN

Over 40 Exercises for Good Hands, Power Legs, and Superior Seat Awareness

Sally Batton

with Christina Keim

Photographs by Amanda Terbrusch
with Ashley Yeaton and Olivia Yossa

Trafalgar Square
North Pomfret, Vermont

First published in 2022 by
Trafalgar Square Books
North Pomfret, Vermont 05053

Disclaimer of Liability
The author and publisher shall have neither liability nor responsibility to any person or entity with respect to any loss or damage caused or alleged to be caused directly or indirectly by the information contained in this book. While the book is as accurate as the author can make it, there may be errors, omissions, and inaccuracies.

Trafalgar Square Books encourages the use of approved safety helmets in all equestrian sports and activities.

Library of Congress Cataloging-in-Publication Data
Names: Batton, Sally, author. | Keim, Christina, author.
Title: The athletic equestrian : over 30 exercises for good hands, power legs, and superior seat awareness / Sally Batton with Christina Keim.
Description: North Pomfret, Vermont : Trafalgar Square Books, 2022. | Summary: "Learn winning Division I collegiate riding coach Sally Batton's time-proven warm-up and her exciting "Equicize" routine: a series of progressive exercises similar to aerobics on horseback. Batton's recommendations help you build and strengthen the major muscle groups used by equestrian athletes, and all exercises can be customized so you can raise or lower the intensity as needed to suit your age, level, and riding style" -- Provided by publisher.
Identifiers: LCCN 2021031922 (print) | LCCN 2021031923 (ebook) | ISBN 9781646010516 (paperback) | ISBN 9781646010523 (epub)
Subjects: LCSH: Horsemanship. | Horse sports.
Classification: LCC SF309 .B333 2022 (print) | LCC SF309 (ebook) | DDC 798.2--dc23
LC record available at https://lccn.loc.gov/2021031922
LC ebook record available at https://lccn.loc.gov/2021031923

All photos and illustrations by Amanda Terbrusch except: 1.2, 1.3A, 1.3B, 1.4A, 1.4B, 1.5A, 1.5B, 1.6, 1.7, 1.8, 1.10, 2.8A, 2.8B, 3.11, 5.11, 5.12, 6.1, 6.15, 6.19A, 6.19B, 6.19C, 6.21, 6.22, 7.8, 7.10A, 7.10B, 7.12, 7.18A, 7.18B, 7.23A, 7.23B, 8.6, 8.8, 8.13, 9.1, 9.2, 9.3, 9.6A, 9.6B, 9.9A, 9.9B, 9.16, 10.2, 10.6A, CONC 2 (by Olivia Yossa); 3.1, 3.7A, 3.7B, 3.7C, 3.7D, 3.7E, 3.7F, 3.7G, 4.2, 5.2, 5.3, 5.4A, 5.4B, 5.4C, 5.5A, 5.5B, 5.9B, 5.9C, 6.4, 6.7B, 6.7C, 6.7D, 6.7E, 6.13A, 6.13B, 6.16, 6.17, 6.26, 7.19A, 7.19B, 8.3, 8.5, 8.9, 8.10A, 8.10B, 9.11, 9.17, Batton Headshot (by Ashley Yeaton); 1.9, 2.1, 3.9, 3.10, 3.13, 4.1, 4.12, 5.7A, 5.7B, 6.6, 6.20, 7.5, 7.6, 7.7, 8.1, 8.14, 9.10, 9.18, 10.12A, 10.12B, 10.18, ACK1, CON 1, CON 4, Cover, I.3, I.4 (by Dartmouth Athletics); 10.5A, 10.5B, 10.10, 10.14, 10.15, 10.17B (by Lori Watts); 7.9A, 7.9B, 7.9C, 9.4 (by Chromepie Photography); 3.2A, 3.2B, 3.2C (by Marin Gilliland); 3.4A, 3.4B (by Denny Emerson); Conc 3 (by Andree Ebell); 10.13, 10.16, 10.17A (by Sophia Arana); 2.9, 10.9, I.2 (by Chromepie Photography); 4.5 (by Eric Schneider); 2.7, 6.5, 6.18, 10.8 (stock photos); Chapter header photos: Introduction, Chapter 10 (Dartmouth Athletics); Chapters 1, 2, 3, 8, 9, Conclusion (Olivia Yossa); Chapters 4, 5, 6, 7 (Amanda Terbrusch)

Book design by Lauryl Eddlemon
Cover design by RM Didier
Index by Andrea Jones (JonesLiteraryServices.com)

Printed in China

10 9 8 7 6 5 4 3 2 1

This book is dedicated to all the horses who have allowed their riders to experience the joy of the human-equine bond.

Contents

5

16

28

41

63

84

108

Introduction

For over 35 years, I coached collegiate equestrians, first at Centenary University in New Jersey, then as head coach of the varsity Dartmouth College Equestrian Team in New Hampshire. Throughout my career, I have seen riders struggle with the same sorts of problems—issues like swinging lower legs, stiff arms, and incorrect mechanics in the jumping position.

What I came to realize is that these fundamental problems happen for two reasons. First, riders often lack a correct understanding of the biomechanics required to maintain their position. We have all heard that "practice makes perfect," but when it comes to rider form and technique, using your body in an inefficient manner only serves to solidify the wrong movements on the horse. Secondly, some riders simply lack the suppleness and strength required to maintain a fluid, elastic position on the horse.

Often, riders are limited in their progress because they do not have the opportunity to ride enough to get truly "riding fit." Over time, these holes in training can lead to frustration—for riders who feel they cannot meet their goals or make progress, and for horses that do not understand what the rider is trying to tell them.

In my Athletic Equestrian training system, I emphasize a methodical warm up and the use of my *Equicize* exercises to help riders overcome these common obstacles. The Athletic Equestrian training system is not just basic conditioning—it utilizes an improved understanding of rider biomechanics and progressive exercises to develop heightened body awareness and improved muscle tone. We cover horsemanship essentials such as the half-halt, correct bending, and the effective use of the rider's aids in transitions to help improve performance. We use two-point exercises to help get lower legs strong and fit. Each Athletic Equestrian exercise has modifiers to lower or raise the intensity as needed.

I have traveled all over the United States teaching Athletic Equestrian clinics to riders of all levels and diverse backgrounds—riders just like you. My Athletic Equestrian training system is designed to help refine and polish all riders, regardless of experience. The Athletic Equestrian training system consistently produces results not only in the show ring but for the recreational rider, helping her to be more secure and balanced in the saddle and effective with her aids.

I will introduce you to some of my favorite Training Tools, including Magic Bands, Pommel Blockers, Wrist Sticks, Fingers-Closed Balls, and Eyes-Up Goggles. No need to go out and buy expensive gadgets at the tack store—these simple tools can each be made or purchased for $10 or less. And I will teach you the *Power Leg*—the number one technique to prevent your lower leg from sliding back during the trot, canter, and two-point on the flat as well as during the approach, takeoff, and recovery from a jump.

I teach my clinics like I taught my practices

The Dartmouth College Varsity Equestrian Team.

with the Dartmouth Equestrian Team—attention to detail matters. For example, before even entering the arena, I make sure all bit pieces are in keepers and saddle pad straps are correctly connected to the billets. Once the rider is mounted, I ensure that stirrup leathers and reins are untwisted. Paying attention to detail is a mindset that you must establish every ride, every time.

I also teach mental toughness. When you ride, your body must do a hundred different things, and if the rider is distracted, it will affect how she rides. I teach riders that to follow a system means that you carry it out in each and every practice, lesson, or training session. I expect my athletes to build on our previous sessions and

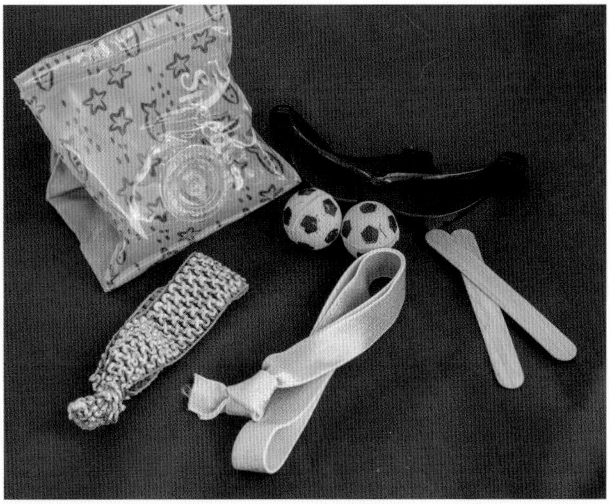

My favorite Training Tools include Magic Bands, a Pommel Blocker, Wrist Sticks, Fingers-Closed Balls, and Eyes Up Goggles.

Emily's horse has the benefit of a relaxed, harmonious rider on his back.

You too can ride like a varsity athlete. Storey and Erin wait for results at a collegiate competition.

use the skills they learned to move on to the next task. By following the training system that I outline in *The Athletic Equestrian*, you *will* see progress in your own riding—and your horse will benefit from having a more relaxed, harmonious rider on his back and holding his mouth.

This book is for the serious junior or amateur who wants to be more effective and use correct body mechanics in order to improve the performance of her horse. It is for the rider who wants to have more fun through better communication with her equine partner. It is for the ambitious rider looking to reliably execute and deliver solid performances in the show ring. It is also for the everyday rider who wants to simply be able to enjoy her horse safely.

I recommend reading through this book in its entirety before beginning to incorporate the exercises and tips outlined into your practice. In doing so, you will recognize how each piece builds on the one before it, as a strong foundation lays the support for the frame of a house. Highlight lines and "dog ear" pages, then take the book with you to the barn. As you progress through the exercises laid out in my system, these marked passages will serve as valuable reminders that *you* can ride like a varsity athlete.

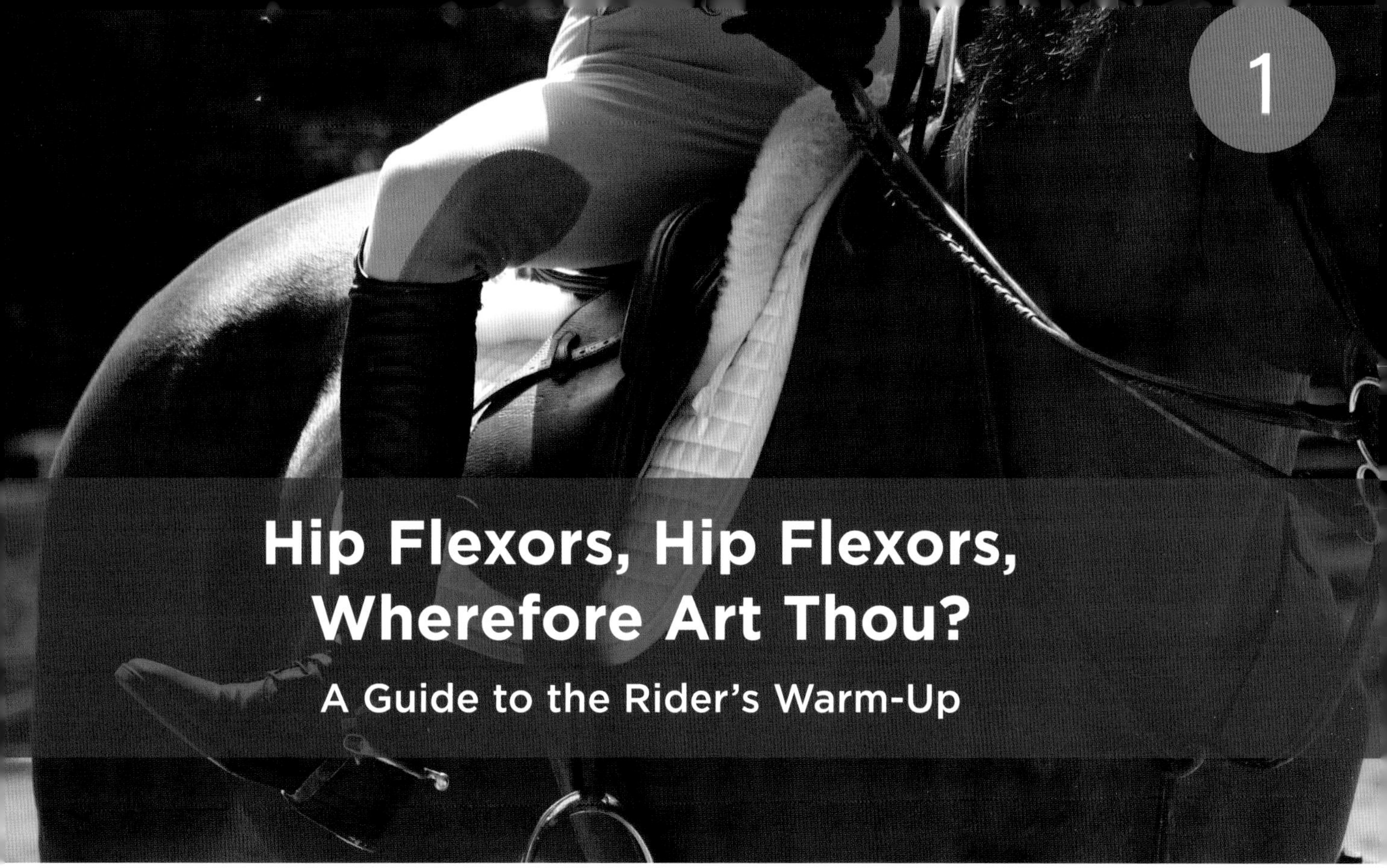

1

Hip Flexors, Hip Flexors, Wherefore Art Thou?

A Guide to the Rider's Warm-Up

While most coaches and riders are aware of the importance of a thoughtful warm-up for the horse, many overlook the need for a systematic warm-up for the rider. This chapter will describe the proper execution of six specific exercises—*Toe Rolls, Soldier Leg Lifts, Froggy Leg Lifts, Knee Stretch Downs, Windmills* and *Shoulder Rolls*—all of which help the major joints, ligaments, tendons, and muscles of the rider to loosen and limber up before more intense work. I have chosen these exercises because they address the most common rider problem areas; can be completed efficiently; and are not too cumbersome for the rider to remember and practice.

These six warm-up exercises serve to both stretch and strengthen the rider's ankles, hips, lower back, and shoulders. When a rider performs these exercises, she is searching for the feeling I call "good stretch." When a rider releases a good stretch, she feels a positive difference in the soft tissue that supports a joint; the hip feels more open, the ankle more flexible, and the shoulders looser.

Performing each exercise with technical accuracy is also critical. If a rider executes the exercises half-heartedly or in a sloppy way, she will not receive the full benefit. If any of these exercises feel super easy, or if you do not feel a stretch at all, take a step back and review the instructions. Each of these exercises should result in the sensation of good stretch for even the fittest of riders. But at the same time, this is not a case of, "If a little is good, more must be better."

Overstretching can cause negative stress and strain on the body and should be avoided. Any kind of muscle cramp is a form of overstretching. When this happens, release what you are doing, allow the limb to hang naturally, and take a few deep breaths. Sometimes it can help to softly massage the cramp, or move the limb in the opposite direction. Once the cramp has subsided, resume the stretch at a lower intensity.

When doing any exercise program, it is important to recognize that each body is unique. I have included downward modifiers for each exercise for riders with previous injury or other restrictions.

In total, these warm-up exercises should take no more than 10 minutes to complete. This coincides with the phase of the ride in which the horse should be walking on a loose

DROP YOUR STIRRUPS SAFELY

It is important when removing your feet from the stirrups to lift the toe toward the top of the stirrup and remove the foot from the stirrup smoothly and without kicking the horse's sides (fig. 1.1 A). Many riders jerk the heel and lower leg back to remove their foot from the stirrup, almost as if they were kicking a soccer ball, then they accidentally hit the horse (fig. 1.1 B). It is worth taking the time to practice removing your feet smoothly from the stirrups at the halt before you progress to doing it at the walk.

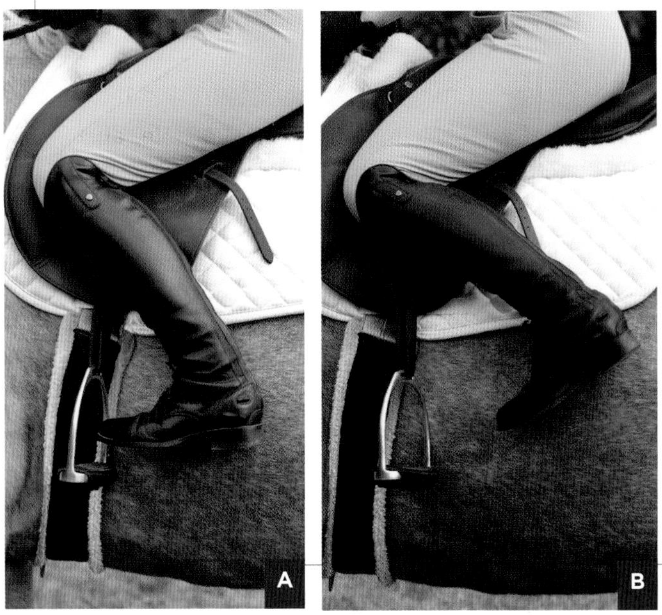

1.1 A & B When Simone removes her feet from the stirrups correctly, she lifts her feet straight up out of the stirrups, then pulls her lower leg back a few inches to remove them (A). Simone F. removes her feet from the stirrups incorrectly (B). She has pulled her feet straight back, which risks kicking her horse.

rein before serious work begins, so the horse and rider will complete the first phase of their warm-up together.

GETTING STARTED

All exercises should be practiced first at the halt to perfect technique. Once the exercises have been mastered, riders should work toward doing all of them at the walk, depending on their ability to balance. To get started, lift your toes out of your stirrups and allow the lower leg to hang down.

Exercise: Toe Rolls

This exercise functions to loosen the ankle joint, allowing the rider to achieve maximum heel depth. Start by removing your feet from the stirrups, allowing your legs to hang down loosely. You are not trying to hold a "leg position" here; instead, focus on removing all tension from the leg, and really allow it to hang down from the hip joint.

To do a correct *Toe Roll,* focus on drawing a circle in the air with your toes in as exaggerated a manner as possible. First, with both feet, flex your ankles and lift your toes up. Next, draw the toes on each foot out to the sides (almost like a duck stance), then point them straight down, then in, and back up. Your left foot will be rotating counter-clockwise, while the right foot moves clockwise. Repeat these *Toe Rolls* 10 times, then switch and do the rolls in the opposite direction 10 times (fig. 1.2).

1.2 Sherry demonstrates Toe Circles, first circling clockwise then circling counter-clockwise.

If doing an exaggerated roll is too much on your ankle joint, start instead by lifting the toe up, then down, to the extent that it is comfortable. Next, point the toe out, then in. Gently repeat these movements 10 times.

THE HIP FLEXOR TRIAD

The next three exercises are used to loosen and open the hip flexors, and are a critical piece of the rider's warm-up. Riders with tight hip flexors tend to grip with their upper thigh muscles, which restricts the flow of energy through the horse's back. Furthermore, the correctness of the entire leg position begins at the hip. When the rider's hip is tight, she will be unable to develop full extension of the leg with the heel lower than the toe. Without a long leg, the rider will struggle to urge the horse forward, create impulsion, and use her directional aids (for example, closing the right leg to turn left or the left leg to turn right).

Each of the hip flexor exercises will be done one leg at a time, making sure you keep your upper body square to the horse's ears and also centered both side to side and front to back. If needed, you can put both reins into one hand and place the other hand on the pommel of the saddle to aid in balance and stability (fig. 1.3 A). When wearing spurs, be sure your lower leg is away from the horse's side for all exercises (fig. 1.3 B).

1.3 A & B Sherry has her reins in one hand and the other hand on the pommel for stability (A). When wearing spurs, make sure your lower leg is away from your horse's side for all the exercises (B).

Exercise: Soldier Leg Lifts

Start by removing your feet from the stirrups, allowing your legs to hang down. Keep the toe and knee facing forward, with your toe lifted. Next, straighten your left leg from the hip until you have almost no bend left in the knee, then lift this straightened leg away from the saddle by engaging the muscles of the outer thigh and hip. Hold for a count of three seconds, then softly lower the leg back to the saddle. Start with five repetitions with each leg, one leg at a time (fig. 1.4 A).

For *Soldier Leg Lifts* to be effective, it is important to build up gradually. Especially in the beginning, only lift the legs enough that you can feel the effort, then release. At first, most riders can only lift their leg slightly away from the saddle. As riders get stronger and more elastic, they will be able to lift their legs

1.4 A & B Sherry demonstrates the *Soldier Leg Lift* with the knee straight and the toes pointed straight ahead (A). She drops her toes down for the *Soldier Leg Lift* modifier (B). Once you get stronger in the lift, you will point your toes straight ahead to increase the difficulty.

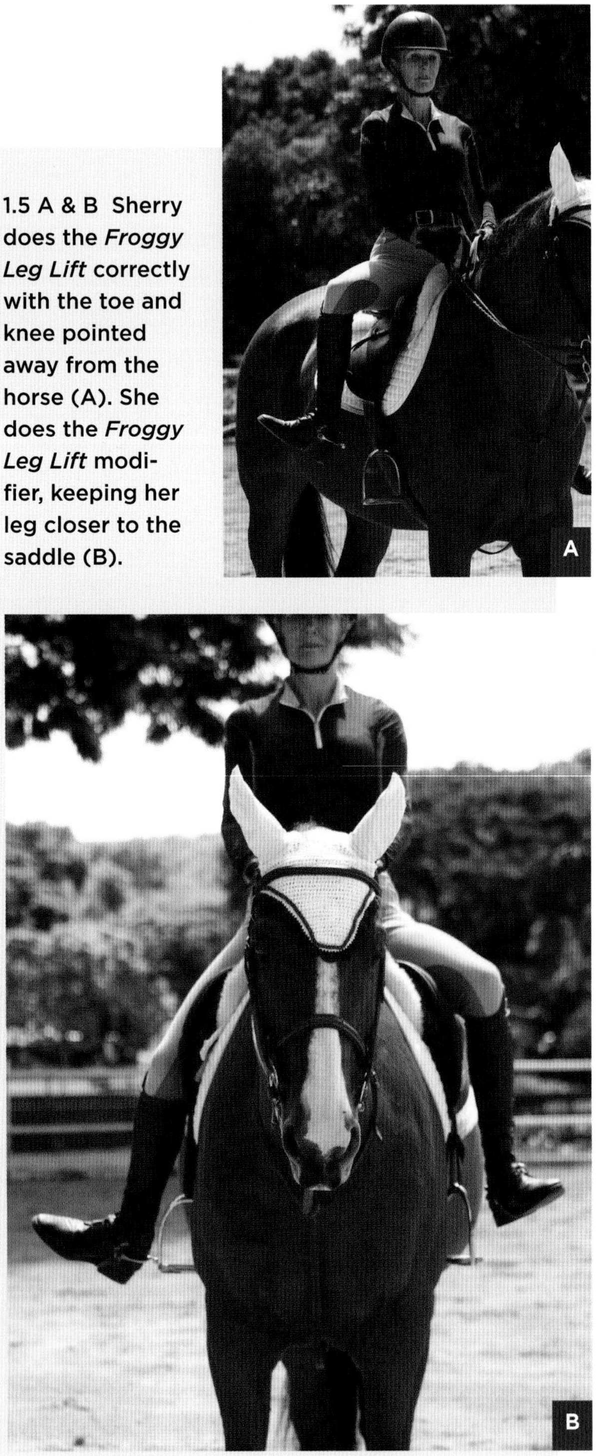

1.5 A & B Sherry does the *Froggy Leg Lift* correctly with the toe and knee pointed away from the horse (A). She does the *Froggy Leg Lift* modifier, keeping her leg closer to the saddle (B).

farther away and with greater ease. Over time, work up to 10 to 15 repetitions with each leg.

Soldier Leg Lifts should not feel easy! When they do, usually the rider has drawn the leg too far forward. If this happens, re-center yourself in the saddle, and think about pressing the back of your knee toward the horse's tail. This will help to reopen the hip angle and will bring the leg back into the correct position. When I am teaching a clinic, many times riders *think* that their legs are straight, and it isn't until I walk up beside them and draw the leg back that they start to really feel the stretch in their hips and gluteal muscles.

To modify the exercise down, either do fewer repetitions at first or allow the toe to drop instead of maintaining flexion (fig. 1.4 B).

Exercise: Froggy Leg Lifts

Froggy Leg Lifts help to activate the quadriceps and increase the elasticity of the rider's hips. Keep both feet out of the stirrups and start with your left leg. Turn the toe and knee out and away from your horse, as if they were pointing west on a compass. Without losing your upper body posture or the external rotation of the hip, use the quadriceps to lift the knee up and hold for a count of three, then lower with control. Start with five repetitions and move to the right leg (fig. 1.5 A).

When *Froggy Leg Lifts* feel too easy, it is likely you have not maintained the external rotation of the hip joint and have allowed the knee to come back toward the saddle. Make sure that the toe and knee remain pointing away from the horse throughout the lift. Long term, the goal is to develop enough suppleness that you can lift your knee higher than your hip, without losing your upper body posture.

When the *Froggy Leg Lift* is too difficult, try keeping your thigh a little closer to the saddle and do not lift the knee as high. You will still get some loosening of the hip flexor, and over time, an increased range of motion (fig. 1.5 B).

Exercise: Identifying Your Seat Bones

The seat bones are two knobby points of the pelvis upon which riders must learn to center their weight at the walk, trot, and canter. I will be referring to the rider's seat bones at other points throughout this book, and for riders who are not familiar with how to find them, the *Froggy Leg Lift* exercise gives you the perfect opportunity.

With your horse at the halt (you may want a friend to hold the reins to ensure he doesn't walk off), put your reins into one hand and your other hand on the pommel. Without leaning forward or back with the upper body, rotate both knees away from the horse's sides by externally rotating the hip joint, as if you were about to do a *Froggy Leg Lift*. With both hips externally rotated and both legs away from the horse's sides, you should be able to clearly feel your two seat bones pressing into the saddle (fig. 1.6).

If you can't feel them, you have most likely leaned backward. Center yourself and try again.

1.6 Sherry does the double *Froggy Leg Lift* making sure to keep her hips square and her shoulders stacked over her hips. This position helps her to identify the location of her seat bones.

Exercise: Locating the Top of Your Pelvic Bone

To do this next exercise, riders will need to know the location of their pelvic bone. Put the reins in one hand, then place your free hand on your waist. Turn your fingers down until your fingertips touch the top of the wing of your pelvis. Memorize this location then return your hand to the reins.

Exercise: Knee Stretch Downs

Keep your feet out of the stirrups and shift your focus to the inside leg. Allow the leg to hang down naturally from the hip, then move the lower leg out and away from the horse's side about 6 inches, while trying to remain soft in the knee and thigh. Imagine that you are wearing a giant pair of spurs, and you don't want to accidentally hit the horse with them.

Next, draw the back of your knee toward the horse's tail until you have an imaginary straight line from the top of your pelvic bone through your kneecap to the ground. Do this with each leg, then simply lift your toes to put them back into your stirrups. I guarantee your leg will feel like it just got a foot longer! Sometimes riders even need to lengthen their stirrups after doing the *Knee Stretch Downs* (fig. 1.7).

1.7 Sherry performs the *Knee Stretch Downs* to fully open her hip and lengthen the leg.

To make the *Knee Stretch Downs* a little easier, increase the degree of bend in your knee. To make it a little harder, challenge yourself to see how far behind the pelvic bone you can draw your leg without tipping forward in the upper body. Make sure that you are always feeling the stretch in the hip, not the knee.

For those of you who compete in either scholastic or collegiate competition, *Knee Stretch Downs* are one of my favorite exercises to do when a rider has first gotten onto her catch ride at the show. Make sure that the horse holder or a teammate is holding the horse's reins!

These next two exercises, called *Windmills* and *Shoulder Rolls,* focus on the rider's upper body, another critical area to loosen and supple in the warm-up phase. Riding in balance requires the rider's head to stay centered over her shoulders and center of gravity; when her shoulders round, the rider's head and neck drop down, causing a negative effect on her

1.8 Sherry puts her reins in one hand and does complete 360-degree circles with the other arm.

balance. The ability to keep the shoulders back also allows for the full range of motion when applying the rein aids.

Exercise: Windmills

Return your feet to the stirrups, and check that your upper body still remains square to the horse's ears, with your shoulders over your hips. Place the reins in your right hand and straighten your left arm, stretching your fingers down toward the ground without collapsing in your rib cage or leaning to the left. Slowly and steadily, lift your left arm forward, up, then back, as if you were swimming the backstroke. Do 10 *Windmills*, always reaching forward first, then up and back. Switch the reins into your left hand and do 10 *Windmills* with the right arm (fig. 1.8).

Windmills open the chest and shoulders

COACH SALLY'S TOP 10 TIPS

Tip 1: Think Positive

No matter where in the world I teach, I have found one universal truth: riders are always their own worst critic. When I ask a rider to tell me one skill she does well and one skill she needs to work on, I get an eight-paragraph soliloquy about her area of weakness. When I remind her to also tell me something good about her riding, she is rendered speechless.

Learning to ride like a varsity athlete takes time and practice. No one, not even the most elite Olympic equestrian, started at the top of the sport. Every single rider who puts her foot in the stirrup and swings her leg over must go through the same process of learning correct fundamentals, building strength, and practicing essential skills. Some parts of the journey will not be easy or fun, but it is important to recognize that the good moments usually outweigh the bad and every day you commit to being just a little better than the day before pulls you closer to your goal.

1.9 Claire's and Sophie's powers of positive thinking often resulted in top placings. At this competition, Claire was the High Point Rider and Sophie was Reserve High Point Rider.

Riders with a positive mindset recognize their strengths and use them to develop the areas in their riding that need further improvement. Being positive doesn't mean a rider ignores challenges; instead, she sees them as short term obstacles that, once overcome, make her a better rider. If she receives constructive feedback from a coach, clinician, or judge, the rider with a positive mindset works to integrate the new information into her practice. She respectfully asks questions when she does not understand, and works every day, every ride, to improve her technique (fig. 1.9).

When a rider with a positive mindset has a tough ride, she doesn't beat herself up about it or allow negative self-talk. Instead, with the help of her coach, if necessary, she will analyze the moments that went well (and why) and those that didn't (and why). The next time she rides, she will be better prepared to make each moment the best it can be.

and help draw the shoulder blades back. Do your *Windmills* slowly and with purpose, keeping your elbow straight and your arm close to the body so that your upper arm is brushing your ear with each rotation. Do not allow your torso to twist as the arm comes around.

If this is too much strain on your shoulders, modify the exercise by keeping a soft bend in the elbow, thereby reducing the range of each rotation.

Exercise: Shoulder Rolls

Continue to maintain your square and centered upper body position, with both feet in the stirrups, holding one rein in each hand. Keep your eyes up and softly focused forward, and chin lifted. Raise both shoulders directly up toward your ears, then draw them straight back, then lower them down. Repeat this 10 times. *Shoulder Rolls* are not just for the warm-up—do them any time during the riding session when you feel tension in your shoulders or upper body (fig. 1.10).

1.10 Sherry does *Shoulder Rolls* to open her chest and press the shoulders back. In this photo, she is raising her shoulders up toward her ears. She will then pull them straight back and then down.

For riders with shoulder issues, modify this exercise by only lifting the shoulders halfway to the ears, or by drawing the elbows out slightly.

In this chapter, I covered six essential exercises that help loosen, stretch, and strengthen the rider. These exercises should be incorporated into your daily warm up, and, once you are comfortable with them, they can be completed while the horse has his initial walking warm-up phase. Remember these exercises are only beneficial when performed correctly; riders should be seeking a feeling of "good stretch" in each exercise. When you have completed them, you are ready to move into the next phase of your workout: *Equicize*.

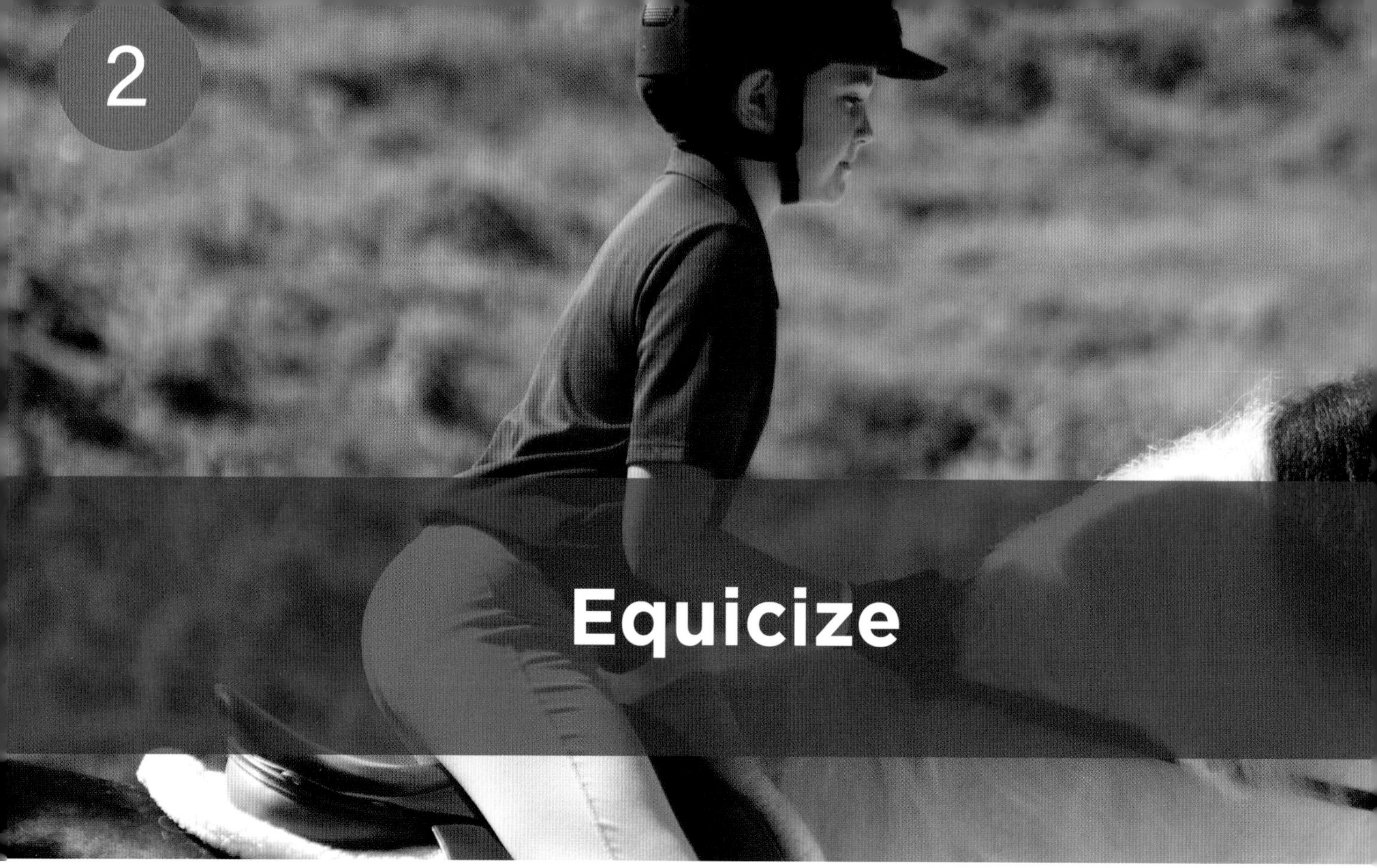

2

Equicize

We all know the best way to get "riding fit" is to find a situation where we can ride multiple horses a day. But for most non-professional riders, this is not a realistic option. The good news is that for the rest of us, there is *Equicize*.

"*Equicize*" is a term I use for a series of progressive exercises I have developed that are best compared to aerobics on horseback. *Equicize* helps to build and strengthen the major muscle groups that riders need to use in order to be secure and balanced in the tack. In particular, *Equicize* helps to strengthen and stabilize the rider's leg, so it remains steady and in position, no matter what the horse is doing. Riders begin their *Equicize* sequence after completing the warm-up stretching and suppling routine detailed in chapter 1 (fig. 2.1). Although a full *Equicize* routine involves numerous levels and exercises, I've chosen to explain the four levels that I used most often when training my team.

Equicize is hard work, but when riders commit to practicing the exercises daily, it delivers consistent results. In addition, *Equicize* challenges riders to develop what I call "mental toughness." I have always been intrigued by elite athletes (like Olympians) and those performing tough jobs (like Navy SEALs). Throughout my career I have studied the mental and physical attributes that enable these top performers to achieve success. I have come to believe there are certain qualities all elite athletes possess; some, such as physical ability, may, at least partially, be determined by genetics, but others, such as mental toughness, are skills that can be learned.

Equicize relies heavily on the *two-point seat* as its foundation. At practices, my team was never just sitting in the saddle. Anytime the horse was on a walk break, they were up in two-point with no stirrups. If they were waiting their turn to jump in a group lesson, they dropped their stirrups and practiced two-point at the halt (fig. 2.2). My team would get so fit that they could canter in two-point with no stirrups—confidently and without pinching their legs.

It all started with developing mental toughness through breaking down each exercise into small enough pieces so riders were able to gradually build strength. By putting themselves under stress and achieving stepping-stone goals, riders develop not just mental and physical fortitude, but confidence in their own ability to complete difficult exercises.

Be sure to give your horse a light warm up in the trot and canter to get his body moving before starting the *Equicize* sequence. You will be working so hard to manage your own body that you won't be able to give your horse much help!

2.1 *Equicize* helps to strengthen the rider's leg so that it remains steady and in position. *Equicize* helps to build and strengthen the major muscle groups that riders need to use in order to be secure and balanced in the tack.

2.2 Anytime you are at the walk or halt, drop your stirrups like Simone T. and go up in your two-point to help strengthen your legs and core. Simone is riding at Jamaica Bay Riding Academy in Brooklyn, New York.

ESTABLISHING YOUR FITNESS BASELINE

Imagine you have decided to take up jogging after a long period of not doing much physical activity. You would never expect to just start off running a 10K; you would start with short, low-intensity jogs and gradually build up

COACH SALLY'S TOP 10 TIPS

Tip 2: Practice Mental Toughness

Mental toughness is one of the single most important qualities in a rider that separates average from excellent. A rider who has developed mental toughness is able to remain focused when she is challenged, whether by the exercise she is doing or by the horse she is riding. In learning to ride, there is a progression of skills and degrees of fitness that all riders must go through. A mentally tough rider has acquired the discipline to not repeat the same mistakes, over and over.

For an instructor, starting from scratch each lesson and reminding riders to demonstrate essential skills they have already mastered is not a logical way to proceed. How is a rider ever going to increase fitness or learn new skills if she keeps making the same mistakes repeatedly?

In my program, I expect riders to remember the concepts I teach them. It takes repetition and muscle memory to accomplish certain riding tasks, but attention to basics such as making sure reins and stirrup leathers are not twisted simply takes discipline. Once a rider has achieved the ability to always rise on the correct diagonal and pick up the correct lead, I expect that with every attempt. When my riders were in a team practice with twisted reins or leathers, or picked up the wrong diagonal, or went more than two strides with a wrong lead, they had to get off and give me crunches!

2.3 Emmaree demonstrates a set of crunches used to develop mental toughness.

This was not meant as a punishment but rather to make riders more aware of what they were doing. If they had to dismount and do crunches while the rest of the class kept going, they were less likely to repeat the mistake. It served as a reminder to practice mental toughness and get it right, every ride (fig. 2.3).

I also want to see grit, fire, and determination. I want to see my athletes using what they've learned during the prior team practice or clinic so we can move on to the next skill. I want to see my riders show up early for their practice or clinic time, mentally prepared for what's to come and ready to work hard in every session. I love it when I teach riders in a two-day clinic and on the second day, they are doing their warm-up exercises and *Equicize* to prepare for the day's work!

distance and speed over time. *Equicize* works the same way. Even someone who rides daily is not necessarily conditioned enough to do the full sequence of exercises at first, and most riders will need to gradually build up to the complete series over a period of time. But how do you know when you have reached your personal limit on a given ride?

The first indicator is your *breathing.* If you start a component of the *Equicize* sequence and fairly quickly either get winded or are unable to maintain a steady flow of breath, back off the exercise and take a short break. I have had riders forget to breathe at all and start to become light-headed. This is a sure sign you need to go back to a more basic variation of the exercise, until you can perform it with enough ease that you are able to maintain your breath.

The next variable to monitor is your *muscle control*. These exercises challenge a rider to maintain her position and balance out of the usual rhythm, and this requires engaging muscles consistently and with greater control than she may be used to. When a rider feels her muscles shaking or is otherwise feeling unable to maintain control of her movements, it is time to back down.

The two-point exercise, in particular, increases the stretch in the tendons and ligaments of the ankle joint; riders will sometimes report a feeling of pressure or pain on their shins, or on the inside or outside of the ankle. When you are experiencing pain, this is a true red flag. Stop what you are doing; if the pain subsides when the extra stretch is released, you may be able to resume the exercise at a lighter intensity. But if the pain does not go away, it is time to consult a medical professional or athletic trainer.

A rider will sometimes feel increased awareness of muscles in her lower back as she spends more time working in two-point. This is actually a symptom caused by her using her back to hold her body off the horse instead of her legs. A rider experiencing back fatigue after working in two-point needs more conditioning in her calves and quadriceps, and must learn to use her legs to support her upper body.

It is also my experience that many riders set their stirrups too long both on the flat and over fences, and this, too, can contribute to

THE STIRRUP LENGTH HACK

To prepare for collegiate or scholastic "catch riding," or any other time you must ride in an unfamiliar saddle, I recommend the Stirrup Length Hack to quickly find the correct adjustment. Here's how it works:

While at home in your own saddle with the stirrups set to your perfect length, drop your irons, and feel exactly where the bottom of the stirrup is hitting your ankle. Be as specific as possible—is it directly on your ankle bone, slightly below, slightly above, an inch below, or an inch above? Figure out where the iron hits your ankle and you'll be able to set your stirrups correctly every ride, no matter what saddle you are using.

FOOT POSITION PRIMER

One of the most common position problems I see in riders is lower legs too far forward. Often, this is the result of trying to force the heels lower than the toes simply by using the calf muscles to press down into the stirrup. The rider is stiff and often in pain. Creating a supple ankle joint that can absorb shock and energy is fundamental to helping riders develop maximum stretch in the tendons, ligaments, and muscles in the leg, and for creating a more effective heel-lower-than-toe position. Deep heels help maintain the rider's overall balance and equilibrium on a moving horse. I compare a rider's deep heels to a tight rope walker carrying a pole; the pole helps the performer to keep her balance by distributing weight across its length, causing the ends to drop down. In the same way, properly weighted, deep heels create stability in the rider.

The key to achieving deep heels correctly is to make sure the foot is properly positioned on the stirrup. First, place the ball of your foot (located between your toes and your arch) on the stirrup pad, with the little toe closer to the outside branch of the stirrup. Next, gently roll the foot so more weight is on the inside ball of foot. When you do this, you will feel more pressure toward the big toe than the little toe. You should also, almost immediately, feel your calf roll into a passive contact position (more on this later) and your heel drop down (fig. 2.4 A).

Throughout your ride, whenever your heel creeps up, correct it by rolling more weight onto the inside ball of the foot, or think, "Step onto the inside ball of the foot." If your foot keeps going back to the incorrect position, or you find it hard to keep the stirrup under the ball of your foot, consider whether your boots fit properly (fig. 2.4 B). Boots that are too big usually cause the stirrup to move closer to the arch of the rider's foot and can compromise her ability to keep weight in the heels.

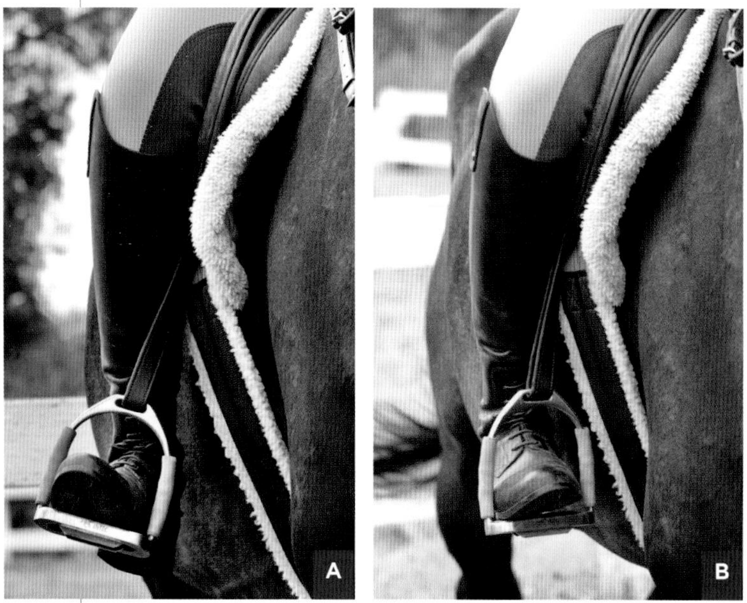

2.4 A & B Rolling onto the inside ball of your foot helps the heel go deeper and allows the calf to rest on the horse's side (A). Rolling your weight onto the outer edge of the foot causes the heel to raise up and the calf to come off the horse's side (B).

lower back discomfort. In the equitation ring, the ideal knee angle is 110 degrees for work over fences and two holes lower for the flat. It is important to practice with stirrups set to the correct length, and it is best to ask your coach or another trusted professional to check the adjustment. Once you know your perfect stirrup length, memorize the stirrup leather numbers for both flat and fences and always set them correctly.

Cramps are a sure sign of muscles that need a break, and when a rider experiences them, she should immediately stop the exercise, breathe deeply, and gently massage the affected area. In general, a rider completing *Equicize* exercises with correctly adjusted stirrups should not experience muscle cramping, but it is not uncommon when she starts trying to do the sequence without stirrups later on.

Exercise: Equicize Level One—Posting Contractions

Increasing body awareness is one of the key principles of my training system, and this first stage of *Equicize* helps riders to become more attuned to those muscles that are engaged and those that are relaxed during each phase of the post. *Equicize Level One* challenges riders to alternately contract, then relax, two muscle groups: the abdominal core and the gluteals. This exercise helps to tone and strengthen each set of muscles.

First, focus on contracting the abdominal core. Establish a positive forward posting trot. During each phase of the post, contract the abdominal muscles by pulling the belly button inward. Without losing your steady breath, continue to hold this contraction for 10 full posting beats. Counting each up beat out loud helps keep you breathing; the last thing you want to do during *Equicize* is hold your breath! After the tenth beat, relax the abdominal muscles.

Next, you ride 10 full posting beats while contracting your gluteal muscles. Imagine you have back pockets on your breeches and you are trying to draw them closer together by squeezing your gluteal muscles. Again, focus on maintaining your steady breath, holding the gluteal contraction through each phase of the post.

Continue alternating between abdominal contractions and gluteal contractions every 10 posting beats for two circuits of the arena.

Exercise: Equicize Level Two—Sit-Ones

Almost every rider can do *Sit-Ones* if they have mastered the basics of the posting trot, and they are a great way to start increasing the intensity of the *Equicize* series. *Sit-Ones* sound easy until you start doing them; a rider must learn to coordinate her own body's movements with the horse's rhythm, then deliberately change the timing of her posting rhythm without losing her balance or count. Most riders will be sweating after just a few circuits of the arena!

To get started, establish a positive forward posting trot, rising on the correct diagonal.

2.5 A & B Simone F. is incorrectly raising her shoulders when she sits one beat to change her posting diagonal (A). She keeps her shoulders pressed down as she sits one beat to change her posting diagonal (B).

Choose a marker on the outside edge of the arena and, as your body passes the marker, count five strides out loud on each *up beat*. After your count of five, sit one extra beat and rise on the wrong diagonal. Post five more strides, then sit one extra beat. Each time you sit the extra beat, make sure your upper body remains square to the horse's ears, and keep your shoulders down. Repeat this sequence for two full circuits (figs. 2.5 A & B).

For some riders, two circuits of *Sit-Ones* every five beats are enough to get their respiration rate up and flush their cheeks. If this is you, take a few laps of regular posting, focusing on returning to a steady breath, then try the sequence again.

If you are still feeling good, you can increase the challenge. Ride two more circuits, this time maintaining a sequence of four regular posting beats and one extra sitting beat. Next, do two circuits of three regular posting beats and one extra sitting beat, then two circuits of two regular posting beats and one extra sitting beat. Finally, do two circuits of ones—post one beat, sit two (essentially, up/down/down/up/down/down).

Riders new to *Sit-Ones* may not be able to go all the way through the sequence from circuits of fives to circuits of ones. Listen to your body and notice when you start to lose the consistency of your breath or the steadiness of your position. This is the moment at which you need to allow your body to "reset" by taking a few circuits focusing on a steady breath and regular posting rhythm (or, in some cases, even coming to the walk).

Exercise: Equicize Level Three—Sit-Ones with Posting Contractions

Once *Equicize Level Two* feels easy—the rider is able to consistently and steadily do two circuits of each count without losing her breath or position—she is ready for the next level of challenge. In *Equicize Level Three*, the rider combines the muscle contractions of *Level One* with the *Sit-One* sequence introduced in *Level Two*. In *Level Three*, riders are challenged to incorporate both abdominal and gluteal contractions into each count sequence.

Returning to the circuits of fives, during each phase of posting, focus on contracting the abdominal muscles by pulling the belly-button inward. During the extra sit beat, relax the abdominal muscles and tighten the gluteal muscles instead. Continue working on this pattern through each descending count (fours, threes, twos). It is pretty hard to contract then release each muscle group in time with the ones, therefore, I do not recommend practicing this pattern in *Level Three*.

Sometimes when the rider is working on this advanced version of *Sit-Ones*, the horse will respond to the changes in his rider's muscle tone by becoming tense himself. When this happens, stop the extra muscle contractions until the horse settles back into a consistent rhythm.

Exercise: Equicize Level Four—The Chest Press

I will go over the two-point more thoroughly in chapter 3; for now, I will assume that riders have a baseline understanding of this seat style. Many instructors use the idea of a deep two-point or cantle touch in their teaching. I call this the "*Chest Press* position." In *Equicize Level Four,* riders alternate between the two-point and *Chest Press* positions (fig. 2.8 A).

The *Chest Press* is like a super deep two-point position—so deep that the rider's chest is almost touching the horse's neck. In *Chest Press*, the hip angle is almost totally closed, the knee angle is deeper than two-point, and the ankles are flexed to the max. When riders try this exercise for the first time, they usually think they are closer to their horse's neck than they really are. Concentrate on closing the hip angle as much as you possibly can, allowing the seat bones to press back toward the cantle. In two-point, I do not allow the rider's hands to rest on the neck, but in *Chest Press*, resting the knuckles on the horse's neck helps riders to find their balance (fig. 2.8 B).

At first, most riders hold onto tension in their muscles and do not fully release their joints to find their maximum fold. Keep focusing on breathing and a feeling of softness in the muscles, allowing the stretch to go through and into the joints of the leg. Experiment with the *Chest Press* at the halt and walk before trying it at the trot.

Once you have a basic understanding of the *Chest Press* position, you begin the *Equicize* exercise. Again, find a positive forward working trot and post with the horse's rhythm. Pick

ATHLETIC STANCE

Being correctly balanced in the *two-point position* is similar to the balance required to do other sports, such as surfing, playing basketball, skiing, or managing a stand-up paddle board. It is all about staying balanced over your center of gravity by maintaining a steady alignment and keeping your joints slightly closed. This is called "athletic stance."

Try athletic stance unmounted. Stand with your feet about a shoulder-width apart, and gently bend your knees and close your hips slightly. Keep your shoulders over your hips, and your hips stacked over your knees and feet. Notice that this position is quite similar to how you might wait to receive a volleyball serve or prepare to shoot a basket. You are balanced and stable but also mobile, ready to spring or jump immediately (figs. 2.6 A & B).

2.6 A & B Simone T. demonstrates a correct athletic stance with her angles slightly closed (A). Then she demonstrates an incorrect athletic stance, with open angles in her ankle, knee, and hip (B). Her open angles will cause her to become stiff and lose shock absorption.

2.8 A & B Teagan demonstrates a correct two-point position (A). She demonstrates a correct Chest Press by keeping her back flat and pressing her upper body almost to the horse's crest (B).

In riding, your instructor has likely emphasized maintaining an alignment from your ear through your shoulder to your point of hip and heel. When you get into two-point, you close the angles in your ankle, knee, and hip, but maintain the hip-to-heel alignment. This is athletic stance on a horse. If your leg is too far forward or too far back, you cannot maintain an athletic stance.

Throughout this book, I will emphasize that the rider must constantly work on her ability to fluidly open and close her joints while maintaining an athletic stance. Picture a surfer riding a wave; is her body standing straight, with all her leg and hip joints open?

Of course not—she would immediately fall off her board. Instead, the surfer closes those angles and gets into athletic stance. As her board travels up and across the wave, the surfer's joints smoothly open and close to absorb the energy of movement. This is exactly what a rider must learn to do—to appear still on an object that is moving, the rider must move just enough to match the horse (fig. 2.7).

2.7 This surfer uses her athletic stance to stay centered and balanced on her surfboard.

To perform two-point correctly, the rider must remain in athletic stance. If you imagine that the horse just disappeared out from underneath the rider, she should land on her feet, angles slightly closed, in athletic stance.

a marker on the outside wall of the arena, and as your body passes the marker, get into two-point and hold for five strides, using the same count rhythm as you did in the posting trot. Next, without sitting, transition smoothly into *Chest Press* position; hold for five strides. Keep alternating between these two positions for two circuits.

I guarantee that you will feel the effort of this exercise right away. If you are not feeling signs of hitting your limit, you can continue and do two circuits of holding two-point for four strides, then *Chest Press* for four strides. Work up to adding two circuits of threes (three strides two-point/three strides *Chest Press*) and then twos.

On the other hand, if you find yourself losing your breath or collapsing onto the horse's neck due to muscle fatigue, take a break from the *Chest Press* and complete a few circuits of posting trot. This will help you catch your breath and give those screaming muscles a break! Once you feel recovered, resume the *two-point/Chest Press* at the number where you left off.

ADVANCED EQUICIZE

The ultimate goal—and this comes only after plenty of practice—is to be able to do *Equicize Levels Three* and *Four* without stirrups. It is critical to understand that this is quite a long-term goal, and to achieve it requires high levels of both fitness and mental toughness. I recommend you keep your stirrups for your *Equicize* routine for many weeks, or even months, before you try it without stirrups. Do not try *Equicize* without stirrups unless you are proficient at work without stirrups in the regular gaits and have developed the balance and muscle memory that is involved in riding without them.

Reaching this level of fitness is not a reasonable goal for every rider; physical limitations from previous injuries or illness, sensitive horses less tolerant of a rider's loss of balance or control, or limited experience working without stirrups in general are just a few reasons why some riders should not push themselves to this level of *Equicize*. But perhaps a smaller goal, such as doing one count of *Sit-Ones* without stirrups, is reasonable. Over time, maybe this can be built upon step by step, until you can complete the entire *Sit-One* sequence without stirrups, and take the stirrups back for the *Chest Press*.

As always, each rider must consider her own current fitness level, her long-term goals, and her unique physical variables when determining personal goals for these exercises.

SESSION GOAL-SETTING

When riders are in a group, whether riding on their own or with their trainer, it can be easier for them to keep going with hard exercises because most of us have a natural desire to keep up with what others are doing. But when you ride independently, it can be challenging to maintain focus and complete the *Equicize* sequence every day. Again, this comes down to developing mental toughness. Set goals for yourself, then break them down into smaller steps. If you are winded on Day One after doing two circuits of five strides two-point/five strides *Chest Press*, make it your goal to do that same sequence every day until it feels easier. When you are no longer struggling to catch your breath, keep going, and add one circuit of fours. The next day, make it two circuits.

I suggest keeping a small spiral notebook in your tack trunk (fig. 2.9). Each day, note how many circuits you did of *Sit-Ones* and *Chest Presses,* and also write down how you physically felt with the number of repetitions. When it comes to *Equicize*, no one can do this work for you. You must develop the mental toughness to do it for yourself.

2.9 Keep a notebook in your tack trunk to write down the number of repetitions each day, and note how you physically felt with each circuit.

3

The Fundamental Two-Point: Gym Squats on Horseback

Many riders only associate the *two-point position* with jumping, so much so that sometimes this seat style is called "jumping position." But the two-point position is really the basis of all rider athlete fitness, so even if a rider isn't interested in jumping, I believe that it is important for her to learn how to do it correctly. In fact, I introduce the two-point to beginner riders at the halt quite early in their education, as it helps them learn how to get their heels down and develop the proper balance needed for all future riding (fig. 3.1). Furthermore, the two-point position helps riders develop better body awareness and strengthen leg muscles.

3.1 Even beginner riders get to try the two-point at the halt. Piper shows how to "ride like a jockey," which puts her up into her two-point position at Floyd Woods Farm in Chester, New Hampshire.

The two-point position engages the rider's calves, hamstrings, and quadriceps, just as practicing squat exercises at the gym would do. The biomechanics of a correct gym squat are virtually identical to those of a correct two-point position, so much so that I often call practicing two-point position "gym squats on horseback."

Ultimately, there are three distinct seat styles that English riders must master: the *full seat*, the *light seat*, and the *two-point seat.* The *three-point seat* is being used when the rider has three points of contact with the saddle—her seat and each leg. However, the term "three-point" is rarely used today, and the majority of my riders wouldn't even know what I was asking for, so I tend to use the term *full seat* instead (fig. 3.2 A). We will discuss the full seat position further in chapter 7 (p. 84).

In the *two-point seat*, the rider has just two points of contact—her legs. The rider's seat is completely out of the saddle and her hip and knee angles close (fig. 3.2 B). The *light seat* is halfway between these two seat styles, when the rider has transferred some but not all of her weight out of her seat and into the legs (fig. 3.2 C). Each style is used at specific moments during a ride for the most effective communication with the horse.

When the two-point seat is correct, the rider will have developed the alignment and balance that serves as the basis for all future work. But many riders have not been taught the proper mechanics of the two-point, and instead of sinking into her leg and closing her angles, the rider stands over or even ahead of

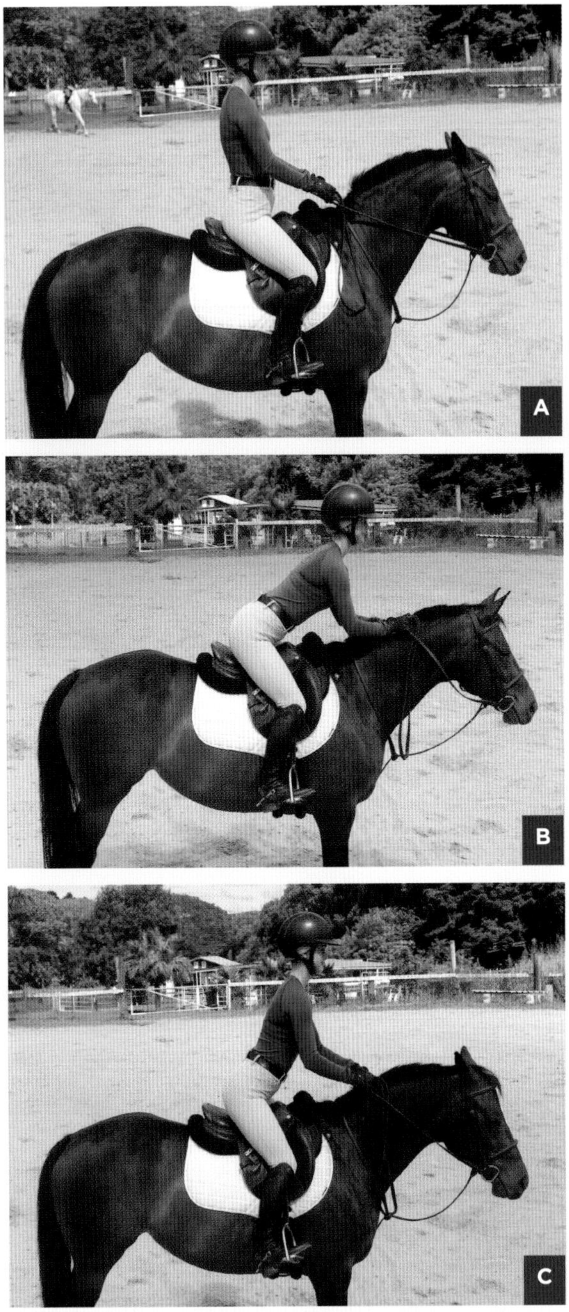

3.2 A–C Teagan is in her full seat with three points of contact between her and the horse: her seat, and her two legs (A). Then Teagan demonstrates her two-point position, with her two legs as the points of contact between her and the horse (B). Positioned in her half seat or light seat, Teagan is halfway between her full seat and her two-point seat with some, but not all, of her weight out of her seat and into the legs (C).

3.3 Olivia M. uses her back to hold herself up in her two-point instead of allowing her legs to support the position while riding at Over the Oxer in Dover, New Hampshire.

the pommel. The rider is then both unbalanced and unable to apply her aids correctly.

In addition, the rider is using her back to hold the two-point, rather than allowing the legs and abdominal muscles to support the position. Riders will often say that their back hurts during or after extended time in the two-point position (fig. 3.3). Generally, this indicates that the rider needs to strengthen her quadriceps and abdominals with exercises completed both on and off the horse to protect her back and execute the two-point correctly.

In this chapter, I will break down the essentials of the two-point into more precise detail, specifically discussing the biomechanics of the rider and the correct action of the hip. I will share my favorite unmounted and mounted rider exercises for developing an awareness of body position in two-point, which will lead to the ability to quickly assess where you have gone wrong if you start to lose your balance, and to fix it on your own. Practicing this important position correctly will allow riders of any discipline to become stronger, better balanced, and ultimately more effective with their aids.

TWO-POINT BIOMECHANICS IN PRACTICE

A rider who can correctly execute her two-point position will be balanced and able to hold the position for multiple circuits around the arena, or galloping cross-country, without worry of falling back into the saddle or onto the horse's neck (figs. 3.4 A & B). In a correct two-point, the rider's leg joints—including the ankle, knee, and hip—are fluid and shock absorbing, and the major muscle groups of the leg (quadriceps, hamstrings, and calves) are engaged.

When I first teach a rider how to achieve

3.4 A & B Denny Emerson demonstrates a classic galloping two-point position (A). Staying centered and balanced off the horse's back aids the horse's balance as he gallops around the cross-country course in eventing. Daryl also demonstrates the two-point position necessary when galloping cross-country while eventing (B).

the two-point, I have the horse stand at a halt in the center of the arena and ask the rider to stand up in the stirrups. Generally, she will stand up by completely straightening her knee and hip joints, almost as if she were standing on the ground. Her open angles make it virtually impossible to maintain her balance (fig. 3.5 A).

Once the rider has felt the instability of standing with open angles, I have her return to the full seat, then ask her to rise out of the saddle like a jockey at the Kentucky Derby. Now, the rider is usually in a position somewhat closer to what I'm looking for in a correct two-point, but typically she is also standing on her

3.5 A & B Stella has incorrectly straightened her knee and hip joints to try and find the correct two-point position (A). Her hip angle is better in B, but she is still open in her knee and is standing on her toes.

toes, causing her to lose balance yet again and pitch forward onto the horse's neck (fig. 3.5 B).

I'll then take her step by step through the three most common two-point mistakes in order to start her onto the path to two-point nirvana—the perfectly balanced two-point position.

The Three Most Common Two-Point Mistakes

When I work with new riders in lessons or at clinics, I ask them to demonstrate their two-point at the trot fairly early in the ride. Almost always, riders will make one of three mistakes, listed here from least to most common: *they have their lower leg too far back, they have their lower leg too far forward,* or *they are simply standing over the pommel.*

Bringing *the lower leg too far back* in two-point is a less common problem, simply because when the rider's leg is in this position, she will find it nearly impossible to maintain her balance out of the saddle. But unless someone has specifically helped her to feel that her lower leg is incorrect, she is usually unaware that this fault is the cause of her two-point problems. Instead, she becomes increasingly frustrated because this leg position causes her to repeatedly fall forward onto the horse's neck, never finding the synergistic rhythm and balance between horse and rider that proper leg position allows. Riders who habitually pinch with their knees, either because of poor balance or weak leg muscles, will often end up with a lower leg too far back (fig. 3.6 A).

Bringing *the lower leg too far forward* is a fairly common problem, and it can be caused by a rider trying to shove her heels down instead of

3.6 A–E Stella demonstrates one of the most common two-point position mistakes with her lower leg too far back (A). Now Stella demonstrates other common two-point position mistakes with her lower leg too far forward (B) and by opening her angles (C). This puts her up and over the pommel of the saddle. Jinae demonstrates the incorrect two-point with open angles over a jump (D) and has "jumped up the pommel" by opening her angles as the horse took off, which leads to near zero shock absorption for her upon the horse's landing (E).

allowing her ankle joint to flex through proper foot positioning in the stirrup and stretch in the calf (see chapter 2, p. 20). This rider, too, will struggle to maintain her balance in two-point, usually falling back into the saddle. Not only is this frustrating for the rider, but it can be painful for the horse, who often receives a jab in the mouth and a slam on his back as a result of his rider's loss of control (fig. 3.6 B).

But by far the most common two-point mistake I see is that the rider *simply stands up over the pommel,* opening the angles of her ankle, knee, and hip. A rider who has learned to execute her two-point this way is never balanced or stable in this position and can even start to look as if she is "posting to the canter,"

THE POMMEL BLOCKER

As with many bad habits, riders who stand up over the pommel in two-point don't usually know that they are making this mistake. As an instructor, I can remind the rider over and over to not open up over her pommel, but her incorrect muscle memory is a powerful opponent. In my teaching, I needed a tool that the rider could actually feel, a tactile reminder to keep her seat back over the saddle, in order to help her to learn a new habit. The solution I came up with is called the *Pommel Blocker*, and you can make one for yourself with materials from your local department store (fig. 3.7 A).

Here is all you need: an inflatable child's sized swim float (I like the ones shaped like a triangle) and a length of self-adhesive Velcro. To determine the right length of Velcro, inflate the float, then take a piece of baling twine or a flexible ruler and run it through the middle where the child's arm would go (fig. 3.7 B).

You will need a long enough piece of Velcro that it can run through the *Pommel Blocker* (fig. 3.7 C), through each "D" ring on the saddle, then connect back to itself on the bottom of the *Pommel Blocker* (fig. 3.7 D).

The *Blocker* should fit snugly to the front of the saddle. If you used a piece of baling twine, clip it at the correct length, then use this piece to measure your Velcro. Apply the self-adhesive backing to your float, and you are ready to put your *Pommel Blocker* to use (fig. 3.7 E).

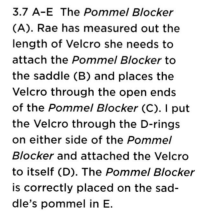

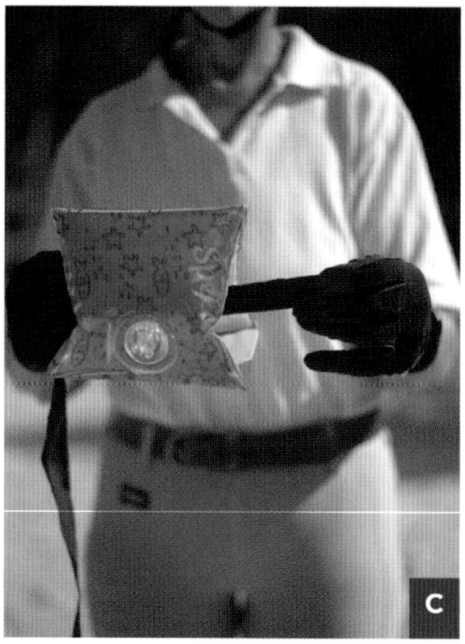
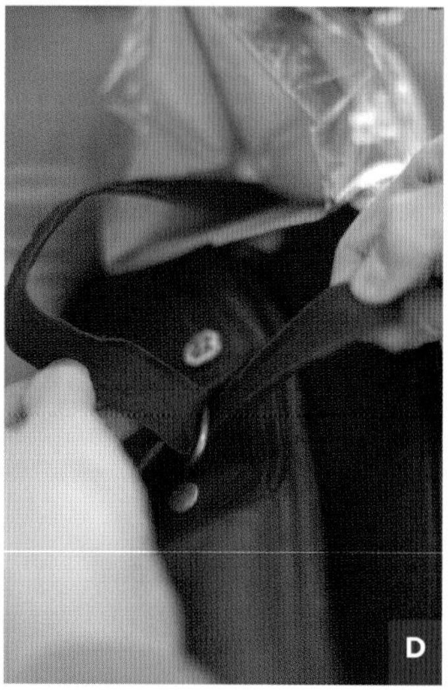
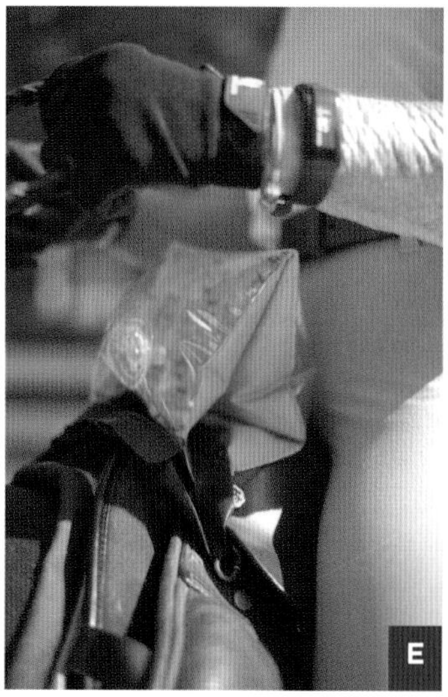

3.7 A–E The *Pommel Blocker* (A). Rae has measured out the length of Velcro she needs to attach the *Pommel Blocker* to the saddle (B) and places the Velcro through the open ends of the *Pommel Blocker* (C). I put the Velcro through the D-rings on either side of the *Pommel Blocker* and attached the Velcro to itself (D). The *Pommel Blocker* is correctly placed on the saddle's pommel in E.

3.7 F & G Rae demonstrates posting too high—a common fault of the posting trot (F). With the *Pommel Blocker* in place, Rae is prevented from posting too high and can learn better body mechanics (G).

Alternatively, cut a piece of clothesline to the appropriate length and use this instead of Velcro to secure your *Pommel Blocker*. Simply run it through the float and the D rings, then tie it in a bow for easy removal.

I can guarantee that with a *Pommel Blocker* attached to the saddle, a rider feels an immediate difference. If she goes into two-point by opening up her leg and hip angles, the rider will hit the *Pommel Blocker* instead, giving her an instantaneous reminder to sink into the joints and keep the seat centered.

Tools like the *Pommel Blocker* should be used long enough to help the rider acquire a new sensation, but then they need to be removed or else they can become a crutch. For a rider trying to develop correct biomechanics in two-point, I suggest using the *Pommel Blocker* for half of the ride, then removing it and finishing the ride without it. Ask a friend to see if she can notice a difference.

The *Pommel Blocker* is also my favorite tool for riders that post too high (fig. 3.7 F). This is a common challenge for new riders, and when I see this bad habit developing, I like to use the *Pommel Blocker* for the full duration of every ride for several weeks (fig. 3.7 G). Once I see that the rider is consistently keeping her post closer to the saddle, I will begin to wean her off the *Pommel Blocker* by starting the ride with it on as a reminder, then finishing the ride without it to see if the correction is maintained.

a major equitation ring fault. Instead of folding correctly and maintaining her center over the horse's center in an athletic stance, the rider who stands over the pommel is stiff and must rely purely on strength to try to get out of the tack. She usually rides with a pinched knee (as the body tries to grip with its strongest leg muscles, the quadriceps) and a loose, swinging lower leg. The worst part is that because she has practiced her two-point in this manner over and over, her muscle memory for the movement is completely incorrect—and she likely has no idea that she is doing it wrong (fig. 3.6 C).

The good news is that with increased body awareness, most riders *can* change each of these incorrect biomechanics (figs. 3.6 D & E). But doing so takes diligence, and sometimes a little help from one of my favorite tools, the *Pommel Blocker* (see sidebar).

TWO-POINT RIDER BIOMECHANICS: EVALUATE YOUR AWARENESS BASELINE

Where do *you* stand on the Rider Awareness Scale when it comes to your two-point position? To find out, try this series of four exercises.

Exercise: Two-Point Test 1

In the first exercise, the rider will exaggerate putting her leg out of position until she develops a kinesthetic sense of how this impacts her upper body balance. Start by getting into your two-point at the trot, then bring the lower leg so far forward that you can see the toe of your boot. You will immediately feel your upper body shift backward to compensate, and you will likely fall into the saddle. Next, try bringing the lower leg too far back.

I haven't met very many riders that can stay off their horse's back for too long when in this position; most people have to put their hands down onto the horse's neck just to stay in the saddle! Practice this exercise until you develop a clear awareness of the position of your lower leg, and the resulting negative effect on your balance with your leg in each incorrect position. Riders who have practiced this exercise enough will almost instinctively know the necessary correction if they experience a loss of balance in the future.

Exercise: Two-Point Test 2

The next mounted exercise requires the assistance of a friend. Starting at the halt in the center of the arena, get into your two-point position, and have your friend place her hand, if you are comfortable with that, or have her hold your *Flat-Back Roll-Up* about 2 to 3 inches in front of the cantle of the saddle. (A *Flat-Back Roll-Up* is a thin magazine rolled tightly and secured with packing tape. The uses for the *Flat-Back Roll-Up* will be discussed in chapter 6—see p. 66). Your friend is now going to try to push you forward with pressure from her hand or your *Flat-Back Roll-Up* on your tailbone. If you have opened the angles of your ankle, knee, and hip, your friend will easily push you onto the horse's neck (fig. 3.8 A). Now, re-center yourself in your full seat and rise into two-point while keeping your friend's hand or the *Roll-Up* in contact with your tailbone the entire time (fig. 3.8 B).

Imagine the feeling of "squatting" while unmounted—your weight goes down into your feet and the muscles of your legs engage. The angles of your leg joints close down and the hip tips slightly. This is the same feeling you are trying to create in your mounted two-point. Keeping this "squat" feeling in mind, your friend is now going to try to push you forward, while you do everything possible to resist her. If you have been successful in sinking down through the leg while rising into the two-point, you won't fall forward. When riders find this correct position, they are amazed at how strong and secure they feel in the tack (fig. 3.8 C).

Exercise: Two-Point Test 3

Finally, have your friend keep her hand or the *Roll-Up* just in front of the cantle, and get back into your corrected two-point. Transition from the two-point seat to the full seat, alternating between them without letting your tailbone break contact with your friend's hand. If you do this correctly, your seat will still be clearing the saddle when you are in two-point position, but it will likely be much closer and more centered than it was before. I tell riders to imagine that their femurs (thigh bones) are pushing their seat bones toward the cantle, rather than thinking about their shoulders coming forward.

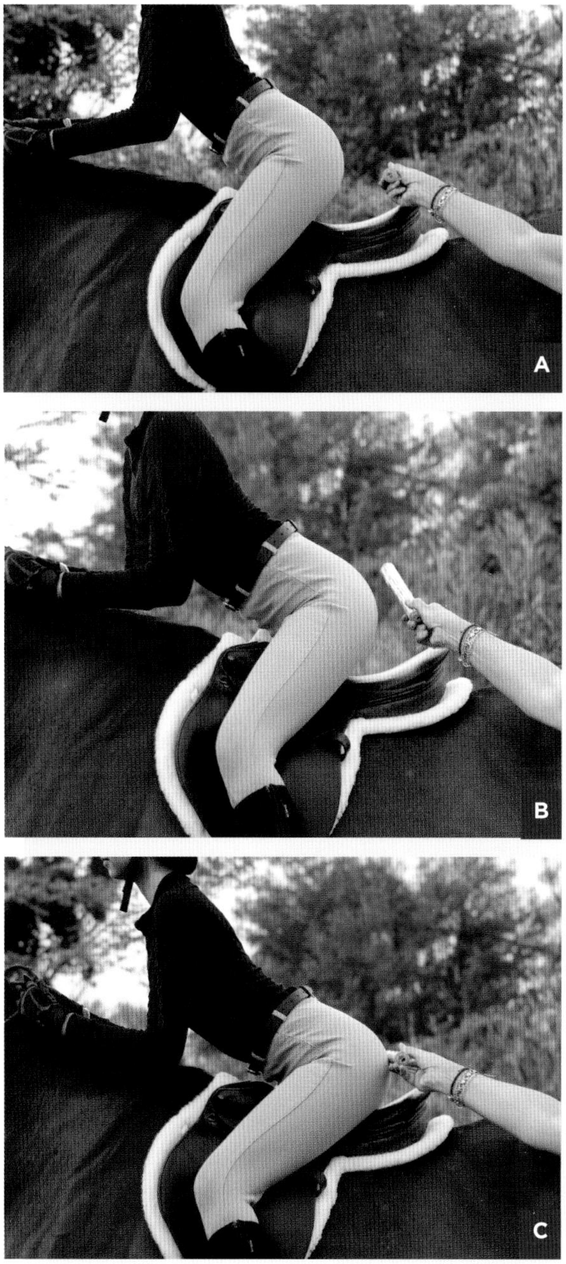

3.8 A–C With Jerianne positioned this far up and over the pommel, I will easily be able to push her forward and off balance with the *Flat-Back Roll-Up* (A). She closes her hip and knee angles to bring her tailbone closer to the *Roll-Up* (B). She is now centered and balanced (C). It will be impossible for me to push her forward and off balance.

COACH SALLY'S TOP 10 TIPS

Tip 3: Dress for Success

When I watch the evolution of a student from casual rider to top athlete, one of the most striking changes is often in how she presents herself and her mount for lessons, clinics, and competition. At busy lesson barns, riders who start off with their hair hanging out of their helmet, no belt, and a grubby T-shirt will sometimes start to emulate the turnout of more experienced riders as their own skills increase; but otherwise, these skills must be taught.

At a minimum, riders should wear polished, well-fitting boots, a tucked-in collared shirt, and hair in a net, even when schooling at home. How a rider appears on the outside reveals the dedication she feels to the craft of horsemanship on the inside. Presenting yourself and your mount in a clean, workmanlike way shows respect for yourself and your instructor, clinician, or judge (fig. 3.9).

3.9 Alex is dressed to impress with her properly fitted helmet, clean shirt and jacket, and black gloves.

However, you don't have to buy the most expensive equipment or model the latest equestrian style trend (even though you may want to) to dress like the rider you want to become. Both tack and riding attire are made in a range of price points to meet the needs of riders at all levels. An entry-level ASTM-SEI approved riding helmet that costs less than $100 is just as safe as a high-end helmet at $500 or more; entry-level saddles are just as functional as their more pricy, custom-designed cousins.

One of the easiest steps a rider can take to look great is to thoroughly and regularly groom her horse. The horse's coat should gleam as a result of routine currying and dandy brushing; a body brush will bring up the oils that create shine. Take the time to pick out the horse's feet, mane, and tail. Don't present to your lesson with a manure stain on the horse's belly or bedding stuck to his flank. Keep manes neatly pulled and bridle paths clipped.

Leather products that are cleaned and oiled regularly not only look better, but last longer as well. Bridles, saddles, girths, martingales, horse boots, and rider boots all should be regularly maintained so that dirt and grime don't build up.

3.10 Suehayla and Bodie are polished and ready to shine at a collegiate competition.

Metal on bit rings, stirrups, spurs, and buckles should be polished to a shine.

Once the tack is on your horse, tuck all the straps into keepers and runners, so that nothing is flapping on the horse. Make sure that your clean saddle pad is appropriate for the day's activity—for example, a baby pad is fine for schooling but not a show—and that it is pulled up into the gullet of the saddle.

Practice keeping your tack and riding equipment clean and organized until this becomes your habit. Work over time to build a small wardrobe of attire that is comfortable and fits well. Keep up with routine grooming so your horse's coat is always one good brushing away from a shine. In this way, even on those days when you are short on time, you and your horse will always be "dressed to impress" (fig. 3.10).

Whenever I do this exercise with riders for the first time, they usually comment on how strange it feels, and they think they are not far enough out of the saddle. But for a jump of 3 feet in height or less, the rider's seat only needs to be about 3 inches out of the saddle (fig. 3.11). If you look at photos of most riders jumping fences in this height range, you will see that many of them are much more than 3 inches out of the saddle. Their upper body is "ahead" of the motion, a serious rider jumping fault that makes the horse's jumping effort more difficult and will result in a point deduction from the judge in an equitation class.

3.11 Teagan and Ruby are in harmony as they go over the Aloha jump at Maunawili Farm in Kailua, Hawaii.

Exercise: Two-Point Test 4

Now that your seat is closer to the saddle, get back into two-point and one more time repeat the earlier exercise, in which your friend tried

3.12 A & B When Emmaree's knee and hip angles are open, Simone T. is easily able to push her off balance (A). When Emmaree's knee and hip angles are more closed (simulating a correct two-point), Simone T. will not be able to push her forward (B).

to push you forward (see p. 37, fig. 3.8 C). With your deeper and more centered balance, she should be unable to do so.

If you don't have a friend to help you try this while riding, you can practice an unmounted variation of the exercise at home with a family member. Standing in an open space on level ground, place your feet about a shoulder-width apart and get into a full squat; slowly reopen your angles until you are about halfway between your full squat and standing positions, and ask a family member to push you on your tailbone.

Notice how this affects your balance (fig. 3.12 A). Next, start to get back into your squat and stop when your angles have closed down enough that you are simulating a correct two-point position. Again, ask a family member to push you on the tailbone and see if she can disrupt your perfect balance. You'll find that in your full two-point/squat position, you will remain balanced and centered (fig. 3.12 B). But when your leg angles are in the halfway open position, your family member will be able to easily push you forward.

4

The Power Leg

A secure, strong, balanced, steady lower leg is the basis for the remainder of the rider's position. Without a strong lower leg as a base, the rider will not be able to engage the core and remain steady on top of the horse. Further, this lack of security will limit the rider's ability to communicate with the horse through her leg aids. Simply put—without a strong lower leg, the rider will never be safe or effective (fig. 4.1).

4.1 With her strong core and secure leg, Olivia C. can stay centered and balanced over the jump.

When I learned to ride, we weren't really taught the right technique to use with our lower legs. Instead, we pinched with our knees and just sort of held on. I still see many riders adopting this approach, and it happens because our thigh muscles are usually stronger than the muscles in our lower legs. It is instinctive—when your brain thinks your body is going to fall, it will tell your limbs to do whatever it takes to prevent that from happening. For most riders, this means pinching with the knees and gripping with the upper leg.

The problem with this for riders is twofold. First, horses are not trained to go forward from a pinched knee; they are taught to respond to pressure from the rider's lower leg, applied just behind the girth. Second, when the rider pinches with her knees, nine times out of ten the lower leg slides back, and when the rider tries to get into her two-point position, the only option is to straighten her knee and hip angles and stand up over the pommel. She is not able to sink into her heel and keep the closed angles in her joints because she has created a pivot at her knee.

The ability of a rider to remain in balance is all about maintaining the correct angles in the leg. Think back to *athletic stance* (p. 24). Closed angles in the ankle, knee, and hip allow you to maintain your ear-shoulder-hip-heel alignment, and to maintain your balance over the horse's center of gravity. Athletic stance allows you to land in a balanced position after a jump. When the upper body is forward, the knee is pinched and the leg angles are open, and the landing phase becomes a jarring impact felt by both horse and rider.

When I teach a clinic, I have the riders demonstrate their two-point for me during the

4.2 When I am ready to teach the Power Leg, I call the riders into the center of the arena and demonstrate the correct two-point position before I go into *Power Leg* detail.

4.3 I have asked Jinae to demonstrate her two-point at the halt. Because she is not balanced, I am easily able to pull her lower leg back.

4.4 Olivia M. demonstrates a correct two-point position at the halt.

warm-up. After watching them for a few minutes, I bring them into the middle and ask them to demonstrate the two-point at the halt (fig. 4.2). I tell each rider that I am going to try to pull her lower leg back, and she is going to try to stop me. Most of the time, I can pull that leg back quite easily, and the rider falls forward (fig. 4.3).

What is the solution? How can a rider practice maintaining her lower leg position all the time, including while in two-point (fig. 4.4)?

The answer is the *Power Leg*.

For many years, watching rider after rider lose her lower leg when she got into two-point position, I struggled to create a lasting correction. But one day, I had an epiphany—back when I used to go foxhunting for hours on end, galloping and jumping and spending most of the time in two-point, I adopted a "leg slightly forward" two-point. I never got tired or felt like I was losing my balance. So, I started teaching this feeling to my riders, and I was surprised to see that their lower legs were no longer slipping back (fig. 4.5).

Foxhunters, eventers, and other riders who have done any type of long-distance work in the two-point position automatically use the *Power Leg* for security, balance, and endurance. The *Power Leg* prevents the rider's lower leg from swinging back on takeoff and over the fence, so when the horse lands, the rider remains in balance and alignment and in her athletic stance.

I have taught the *Power Leg* to hundreds of riders in several countries, and once they have

4.5 Ann's lower leg is slightly forward in her two-point, a position that gives her greater security while foxhunting.

gotten used to the new feeling, every single one comes back to me and says that it feels so much easier. The power comes from being in balance with the horse, every stride, and knowing that you will land totally centered and balanced, seat toward the saddle, ready for the next jump.

So, how do you develop the *Power Leg*?

First, imagine that your calf muscle has three zones: Zone 1 is the straight inside of the calf. Zone 2 is the belly of the calf muscle. Zone 3 is the back of your lower leg. Most of the time, when the rider's leg is hanging against the horse's side with a neutral contact, Zone 1 is touching the horse (fig. 4.6).

Usually, a Zone 1 leg has *passive contact*, meaning that the muscles are only applying enough tension to hold the leg in position. A Zone 1 leg can become active by allowing the toe, knee, and hip to softly externally rotate, applying pressure against the horse's side. This is an *active contact*. When the horse responds, the pressure stops and the leg goes back to neutral. We use this lower leg position frequently on the flat to tell the horse to go forward or sideways (fig. 4.7 A).

This is not your *Power Leg*.

To find the *Power Leg,* slide the leg just a tad forward, usually no more than an inch, and softly rotate it slightly out, until the contact becomes stronger in Zone 2. Really feel the belly of the calf muscle as it maintains passive contact with the horse. Go play with the two-point position in the trot and canter while keeping a stronger than usual contact with Zone 2 (fig. 4.7 B).

This is the *Power Leg*.

Power Leg is not just turning the toe out and riding off of Zone 3. In fact, there are few occasions when Zone 3 is used, perhaps only when really driving a horse forward to an imposing fence or while riding out in the open. If the rider only rotates the toe out and does not increase the contact at the belly of the calf in Zone 2, she will lose the effectiveness of her whole leg (fig. 4.7 C).

My riders use *Power Leg* both on the flat and over fences. On the flat, they can use the *Power Leg* to steady their lower leg at both the trot and the canter, especially on a horse with a lateral canter (sometimes called a "four-beat canter"), or any time the rider feels her lower leg swinging (figs. 4.8 A & B). Over fences, my riders use *Power Leg* on the approach to each fence and in the air. Their knees softly rotate off the saddle, and the seat stays centered instead of coming ahead of the pommel. In fact, you can use *Power Leg* around an entire course, because you can still use your Zone 1 leg in the normal way.

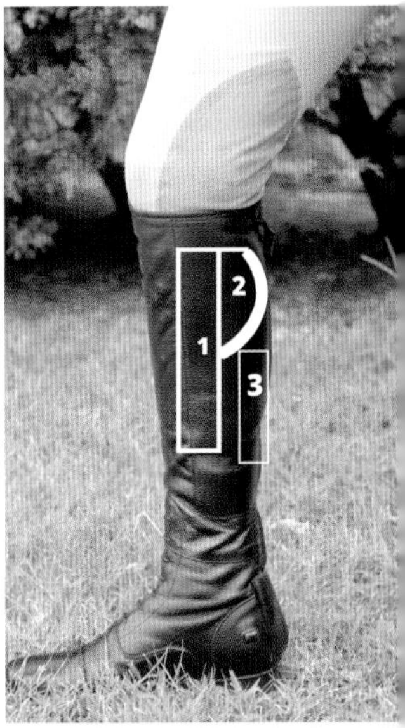

4.6 The zones of the lower leg.

4.7 A–C The lower leg in Zone I, which can apply pressure to tell the horse to go forward or sideways (A). Olivia M. has rotated her lower leg onto the belly of the calf muscle (B). This is the *Power Leg.* Now she has rotated her lower leg too far onto Zone 3 (C). The back of the calf is rarely used.

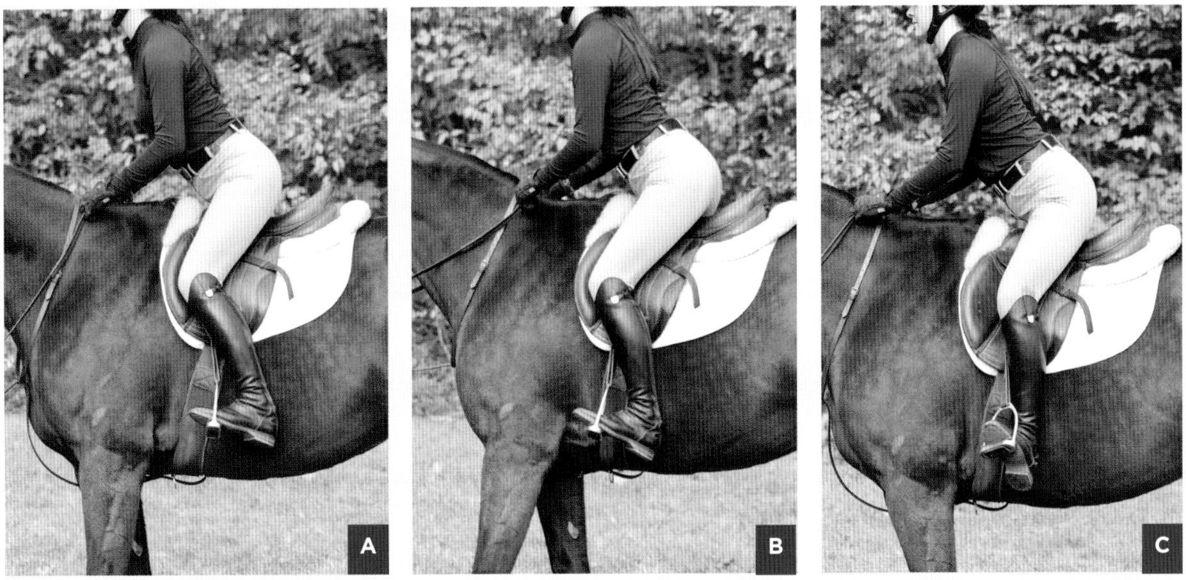

4.8 A & B Olivia M. holds her *Power Leg* in the rising trot (A). The *Power Leg* helps to stabilize the lower leg and prevent it from swinging. She positions her lower leg in the *Power Leg* for stabilization at the canter (B).

THE HORSE'S "GO" BUTTON

A horse that has been properly sensitized to the rider's leg aids will respond best when those cues are given in the correct location. A rider on a sluggish horse can squeeze until it feels like her legs are about to fall off, but if she is not applying pressure in the area where the horse has been trained to respond, the cue is akin to spinning your wheels in the mud.

The horse's *"GO" Button* is a small rectangle, located just behind the girth and under the rider's seat, which serves as the horse's accelerator (fig. 4.9). All leg aids to send the horse forward must be applied in this location or the horse is unlikely to answer them. This is one of many reasons why developing a consistent and steady leg position is so important. When our legs slide too far back or too far forward, at best our horse ignores us and at worst we irritate him to the point where he begins to kick out or buck.

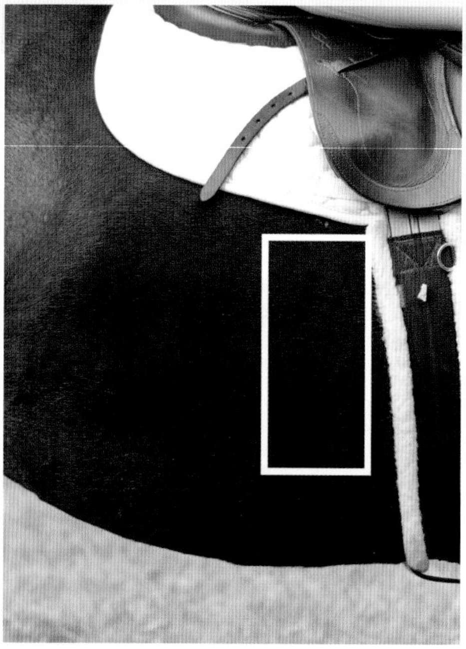

4.9 Horses are trained to respond to pressure in the area behind the girth. When the rider's leg is not in the correct position, she can squeeze all day and the horse will not respond.

Occasionally, riders can take *Power Leg* too far, bringing the lower leg too far forward, bracing in the stirrup, or getting too straight in the knee. Remember that *Power Leg* is much more subtle than that—it is sliding the lower leg no more than one inch forward, while rotating onto Zone 2 of the calf.

So now comes the million-dollar question: How can I "test" my *Power Leg* to make sure I'm maintaining Zone 2? The following exercise will challenge your ability to find the *Power Leg* in the halt, walk, and trot.

Exercise: Find Your Power Leg

At the halt, find a contact with your calf in Zone 2, then sit back into the saddle and return to Zone 1. Cue your horse to walk, and when he moves off, go up into your two-point position. Slide the leg forward no more than one inch, then softly rotate the knee and calf until your leg is back in Zone 2. Hold your two-point and walk around the arena. With your *Power Leg*, you should feel

4.10 A & B In A, the lower leg is too far forward for the horse to receive the signal to move forward. In B, the lower leg is now on the "GO" Button, and the horse moves forward off the leg.

Don't believe me? Try this easy test. While standing at the halt, push your leg too far forward, close your leg, and ask the horse to walk (fig. 4.10 A). Be sure to only use your leg; do not encourage the horse to move by clucking or kissing with your voice or pushing with the seat. No matter how hard you squeeze the leg, when pressure is applied from this position most horses will simply remain at the halt.

Still not convinced? Take your lower leg off the horse and pinch with your knees as hard as you can. Again, most horses will remain perfectly still.

Now, move your leg 2 inches back until it is positioned over the rectangle and give a gentle squeeze. Your horse will easily move off (fig. 4.10 B).

centered and balanced. Practice this transition between halt and walk until it feels natural.

Next, try it in the trot. Ask your horse for the transition, then go up into your two-point and move to your *Power Leg*. You should remain centered and balanced, not falling to the front or back of the saddle. When the *Power Leg* is correct, you will feel so secure that you could stay in the middle of the saddle even if your horse takes a misstep or spooks.

When *Power Leg* feels easy in the walk and trot, you can try it in the canter or even gallop. When the *Power Leg* is correct, you'll feel like your legs are supporting your body above the horse instead of feeling as if your back muscles are pulling your body up.

Once you've mastered the *Power Leg* on the flat, you can test it over ground poles set around the arena. Keep your *Power Leg* in the Zone 2 position for all of the canter work and the work over the poles. The best way to make sure that your leg won't slide back is to always maintain the *Power Leg* position.

Exercise: Power Leg Test

A good way to test your *Power Leg* is to get into two-point position and have a friend try to pull your lower leg back, first while you hold it on Zone 1, then when it is in the *Power Leg* position. The helper should stand to one side of you, facing your leg. Have her place her hand on the front of your shin and pull back toward the horse's tail. When your *Power Leg* is correct, she should not be able to move your lower leg out of position (figs. 4.11 A & B).

Power Leg is one of the most effective tools I know to maintain a correct lower leg position. Riders who have the ability to move their leg from Zone 1 to Zone 2 and back, who can effectively find their *Power Leg* at all gaits and over fences, will experience an increased degree of control and confidence. Because the rider's leg position is the "foundation" upon which their correct position is built, the *Power Leg* is perhaps the single most important aspect of my system for you to master.

4.11 A & B To test your *Power Leg,* first place your leg into Zone 1, then ask a friend to try and pull your lower leg back. Here you can see what happens: the leg easily loses position and falls back (A). When the leg is placed into the Zone 2 *Power Leg,* your friend will be unable to pull your leg back (B).

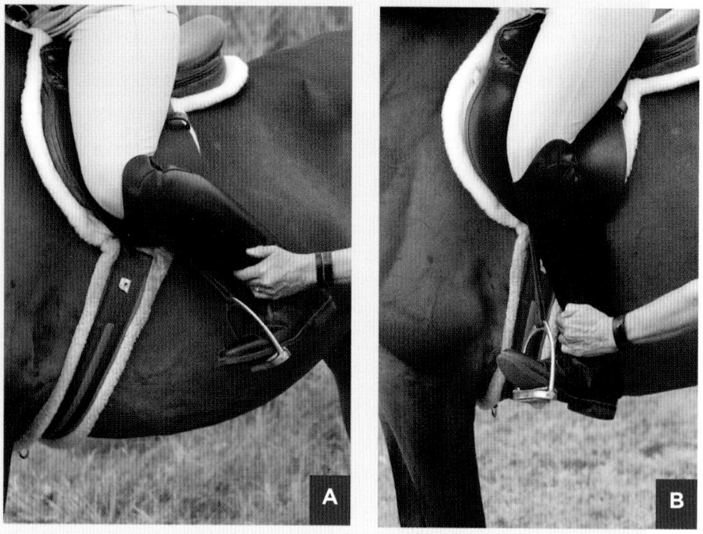

COACH SALLY'S TOP 10 TIPS

Tip 4: Ride with Confidence and at Show Attention

Many equitation judges have told me that they are working on ranking the class in the arena before them from the very first transition to trot. The rider whose number goes to the top of the card draws the eye of the judge not just for her correct angles, deep heels, and effective aids, she is also riding with confidence. Confidence comes from success, and success is experienced when a rider completes daily tasks (such as *Equicize*—see chapter 2, p. 16) with increasing proficiency, or when she executes a complicated exercise by breaking it down into smaller, achievable steps. Confidence becomes a value that effective riders live every day.

If you are a dedicated rider-athlete, the way you carry your body sends a message. Confident riders keep their eyes up, posture tall, and position strong. The last thing you want is to appear to a judge or a coach as being less skilled than you truly are because your shoulders are slouched, your heels have crept up, or you have collapsed a hip. Such body language gives the impression that a rider doesn't care, even when the truth is something quite opposite.

I always had my team riders, whether riding in a lesson or on their own, practice riding at "show attention" (fig. 4.12). This meant that any time they were on a horse, my riders were never slouching, gabbing, or wandering aimlessly around the arena. They didn't ride with long, sloppy reins or incorrect foot position in the stirrup. No matter what they were practicing, I had them imagine that the judge's eye was on them all the time. When you ride like this at home, it will become your habit; when you are in the show ring, there is no change from your normal routine.

4.12 Meghan is riding at show attention and with confidence. Her eyes are up, posture tall, and position strong.

In the final line-up of a flat class, my riders stood out because they maintained show attention. They looked straight ahead, with shoulders back, demonstrating a correct balanced position until the moment they were asked to dismount by the announcer or exited the arena.

In the show ring, it is easier to move down the judge's card than up once she has started ranking the class. To ensure that your number starts at the top of the judge's card and stays there, practice riding with confidence and show attention every day.

5

Good Hands and Magic Bands: Addressing Connection

Maintaining the correct angles of the rider's hands and elbows is essential in order to develop a compassionate connection with the horse's mouth. Additionally, the proper angles will allow the rider to correctly use the elbow, instead of the wrist or fist, during transitions.

Horses may seem like they are too strong and powerful for something as seemingly small as the angle of a rider's elbow or the position of her wrist to affect them in a negative way. But horses are extremely sensitive and notice any source of tension in the rider's body—even if the tension is in her pinky finger. To be effective, riders must learn to ride from their flexible elbows while maintaining correct alignment of the wrists.

Riding with flexible elbows means that the rider can bring her elbows toward her own pelvis, or even past it, by holding with an engaged core. She can move with and follow the horse's head and neck in each gait, without pulling or tugging, but also without letting go of the reins. This ability is fundamental to creating connection with the horse's mouth (fig. 5.1).

In a correct and effective position, the rider's upper arm should be hanging loosely by her side, her elbow bent to 90 degrees, with her fingers softly closed in a fist around the reins, such that the tips of her fingers touch her palms. The wrists should be slightly curved out. Imagine a small bouncy ball held between the wrists; their curve should match the contour of this ball (fig. 5.2).

Unfortunately, most riders keep their arms too straight, riding only from their fists. When the elbows are straight and the wrists drop down, the rider loses the flexibility of the elbow and the elasticity in her connection with the horse. Her own body gets in the way of the correct use of the rein aids. Habits like these often become completely ingrained in a rider's practice and can be hard to overcome (fig. 5.3).

I mentioned earlier that if a rider has tension in her pinky, the horse can feel it. When it

5.2 The correct hand position means fingers closed to touch the palms with a slight, outward curve in the wrists.

5.1 Simone T's flexible elbow shows her soft, flowing connection to her horse's mouth. She can move with and follow the horse's head and neck, which is fundamental to creating connection with the horse's mouth.

THE EFFECT OF THE BIT ON THE HORSE

I am always surprised by how few riders really understand how the bit works in the horse's mouth, and how the strength of the bit they are using should influence their rein aids. Depending on the style of bit, when the rider pulls on the reins, the horse may feel pressure not just on his bars but the corners of his lips, his tongue, the roof of his mouth, the poll, and/or the chin groove.

The effect of these pressure points adds up, and when the rider is operating under the assumption that the hand alone makes the horse stop, she usually uses too much strength in applying her rein aids.

It is beyond the scope of this book to break down the many variations of bit style, but in general terms, it is important to understand that if a rider's elbows are locked straight or her wrist angle is incorrect, even the effect of a simple snaffle will be magnified. At best, the horse may toss his head to avoid the extra tension of the bit, but at worst, the rider's bad habit can create long-term connection problems in the horse or cause him significant discomfort.

Learning to compassionately use the bit as a tool of tactful communication is one of the most important aspects of becoming a true horseman. One of my favorite images is to picture that instead of a bit, the rider has just a piece of thread in the horse's mouth. To not break the thread requires precise control of the pressure through the reins. My ultimate goal is for a rider to have not more than about 5 pounds of weight in each hand throughout her ride. When using the elbow to give a rein aid, that weight may increase to as much as 10 pounds, just for a moment, before returning to 5 pounds again.

5.3 Kendall's elbows are straight, causing her to lose her flexible contact with her horse's mouth.

comes to wrist position, it should make sense that significant flaws such as "piano hands" (wrists held flat, fig. 5.4 A), "puppy paws" (wrists held face down and bent, fig. 5.4 B), or wrists popped in or out (fig. 5.4 C) will all lead to tension in the horse. Riders with incorrect wrist position cannot use their flexible elbows correctly, if they are even able to maintain the elbow angle at all. Instead of softness and energy absorption, flexibility, and effectiveness, these wrist faults will cause the rider's connection with the horse to be stiff and unsympathetic. Just as with straight elbows, incorrect wrist position can become a thoroughly ingrained bad habit that takes some diligence and patience to correct.

It is important to note that one rider flaw

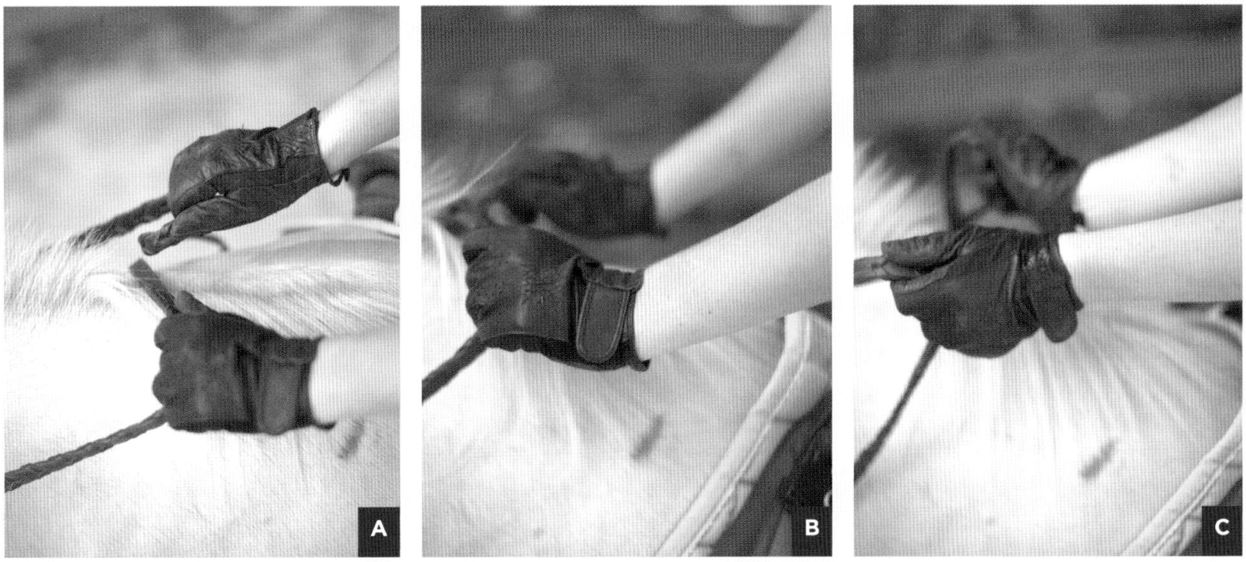

5.4 A–C "Piano hands" with the palms turned toward the ground (A), and "puppy paws" with the palms turned toward the ground and the wrists also breaking downward (B). Wrists broken inward will cause tension on the horse's mouth and create issues with correct use of the reins (C).

doesn't necessarily cause the other. I see riders with correct wrist position and straight elbows, and riders with elastic elbows who break at the wrist. But each of these rider faults will have a negative effect on her connection with the horse. What is especially unfortunate is that when the horse tries to escape the rider's insensitive hands, some trainers will simply prescribe a stronger bit, rather than addressing the true source of the problem.

Let's pause here and think about how most of us were first taught how to ride. Usually, novice riders are told only that the hands make the horse stop, and the legs make the horse go. They are not taught the mechanics of the correct use of the rein, or the importance of maintaining an elastic elbow held at a 90-degree angle. Without this understanding, it is no wonder that instructors see so many riders holding their elbows straight.

Sometimes, riders keep their elbows straight because they think they are being soft on the horse's mouth. Maybe the rider's instructor told her that she needed to "give," and in response she pushed her arms out in front of her like a version of Frankenstein's monster. But because the horse's head and neck oscillate (especially in the walk and the canter), if the rider's arms are shoved forward with a stiff, locked elbow, the horse's mouth will be jabbed by the bit almost every other beat. The rider isn't moving in a way that promotes being soft on the horse's mouth; in fact, she is doing the exact opposite.

ELBOW MAGIC BANDS

When I first tried to help riders correct the angle of their elbows, I tried the age-old technique of having the rider use her elbows to hold a dressage whip behind her back (fig. 5.5 A). But I found that a dressage whip was too flexible to effect a true correction, and some horses were bothered by the lash. I tried riding crops, which were stiffer but usually too short. Next, I had my students use wooden dowels, but these were uncomfortable for the rider, sometimes causing back problems—plus most school horses are quite nervous to see someone approaching them with a wooden dowel in her hand (fig. 5.5 B)! I needed a tool that was both rider- and horse-friendly, something strong enough to help increase the rider's awareness of her elbow angle but also safe enough that it would easily release if a problem arose. My solution is the *Elbow Magic Band.*

The *Elbow Magic Band* is easy to make at home. All you need is a 3-foot length of 1-inch-wide elastic from your local craft store. Make sure to choose elastic that is fairly stretchy, rather than the style that is thicker and stiffer. This stretchy elastic will let the *Band* do its job (making the rider aware of her elbow position), but if she gets in trouble and needs to use her arms, the *Band* will just roll off her elbows and not impede her control of the horse (fig. 5.6 A).

To make your *Band,* hold the two ends of elastic together and tie a knot about 3 inches from the ends (fig. 5.6 B). You will now have a loop, or band, of elastic material. To adjust the knot to the perfect setting for your body, put the

5.5 A & B A dressage whip is placed through Kendall's elbows to encourage a bent elbow (A). A wooden dowel is placed through Kendall's elbows to encourage bent elbows but is uncomfortable and may spook the horse should it break (B).

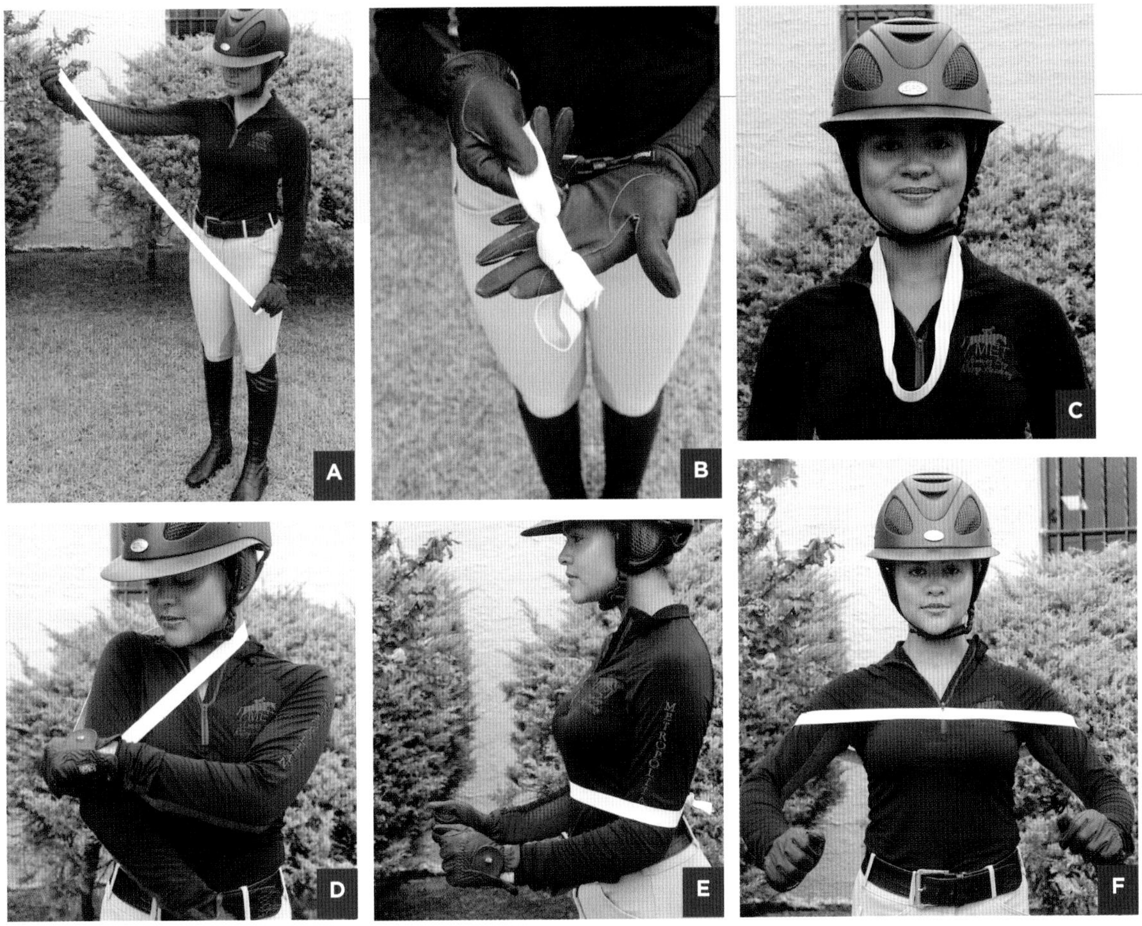

5.6 A–F Cut a 3-foot-long piece of 1-inch-wide elastic (A). Make sure you use elastic that is stretchy, not stiff. Tie the ends of the elastic together to make your *Elbow Magic Band* (B). Place the *Elbow Magic Band* around your neck (C). Pull the *Elbow Magic Band* down over each shoulder (D). Correct placement of the *Elbow Magic Band* in the creases of each elbow (E). We use stretchy elastic so that, in case of emergency, the *Elbow Magic Band* will release from the elbow creases (F).

Band over your head like a necklace (fig. 5.6 C). Use your right hand to pull the left side of the *Band* down over the left shoulder until it rests on your elbow crease, then use your left hand to tug the *Band* down around the right elbow, until it is sitting in both elbow creases (fig. 5.6 D). The *Band* should be tied tightly enough that you are aware of its presence, but not so tightly that you cannot move your elbows out and away from the sides of your body at least 4 inches.

When you keep your arms in the correct position, the band effortlessly stays in place, and you will feel the elastic on the inner crease of your elbows (fig. 5.6 E). But if you open and straighten your elbows, the band will work its way up your biceps, immediately alerting you to the change in your elbow angle (fig. 5.6 F). If this happens, stop and pull the *Band* back down into the correct position before continuing your practice.

5.7 A & B Claire has the correct elbow angle to follow a low head carriage (A). Claire is now on a horse with a high head carriage, so she needs to raise her hands to maintain the line from her elbow to the horse's mouth (B).

In order to break this bad habit, and to create the elastic, empathetic elbow that will promote compassionate, correct connection with the horse's mouth, I use one of my favorite Teaching Tools—the *Elbow Magic Band* (see sidebar). I love this tool so much that I use it on every rider I work with.

For riders with wrist position issues, or for those who seesaw on the bit or hold their hands unevenly, I will add a smaller variation, the *Wrist Magic Band*. *Wrist Magic Bands* can be used on their own or in conjunction with *Elbow Magic Bands*.

As with all of my Teaching Tools, a rider should use the *Elbow Magic Band* for a period of her ride, then remove the *Band* and practice maintaining the correction on her own. I find that creating lasting change in a rider's elbow angle takes time and patience; she may have to ride with the *Elbow Magic Band* for several months before the new habit becomes consistently established. But perhaps one of the most powerful motivators will be the response of the horse. The more consistent the rider becomes in maintaining her 90-degree elastic elbow, the softer the horse will become in his jaw and poll.

I want to pause here and talk about one other variable that can challenge the rider in keeping her elbow angle correct, and that is the horse's head carriage. I work with English riders across the disciplines, and there are some lovely riding horses that naturally have either a higher or lower head carriage, which can make it more difficult for the rider to easily maintain the traditional straight line from the horse's mouth to her bent elbow. For example, riders of breeds with a naturally long-and-low head carriage, such as Quarter Horses, often not only have their hands too far forward with a too-straight elbow, but they also open their fingers in an attempt to be soft and following (5.7 A). Riders of horses with a high head carriage, such as Morgans or jumper-type animals, may be good at keeping a bent elbow, but they also become too accustomed to riding on a super-short contact and with their hands too high (5.7 B). In both cases, the rider is certainly not helping the horse, and is more likely interfering.

SHORTENING YOUR REINS—CORRECTLY

A rider must adjust her rein length throughout her ride to suit the variables at hand, including her horse's head carriage and the gait he is traveling in. Lengthening the reins comes easily for most, as the rider just needs to loosen her grip on the reins slightly. But when it comes to shortening the reins, I meet many riders who do so by "creeping" their hands forward. These riders loosen the fingers of both hands simultaneously, then "creep" their grip toward the horse's mouth, barely advancing their contact at all. Not only is this completely inefficient, but the process is so slow that the horse often takes advantage of the loosened reins to yank down and pull them even farther out of the rider's hands!

✳ Exercise: Shorten Your Reins ✳

To shorten your reins CORRECTLY, try this:

To shorten the left rein, take your right hand and touch your right thumb to the knuckle of your left thumb, keeping your other fingers closed around the right rein (fig. 5.8 A).

Put the pad of your right index finger on your left rein to secure it in place, then slide your left hand toward the horse's mouth the required distance (fig. 5.8 B).

To shorten the right rein, repeat the process but reverse the hands (figs. 5.8 C & D).

USING THE ELBOW AND WRIST MAGIC BANDS

For the rider on a horse with a naturally low head carriage, I will absolutely suggest the use of the *Elbow Magic Band* to help establish the correct elbow angle. But she will also need to work on strengthening her core, because if

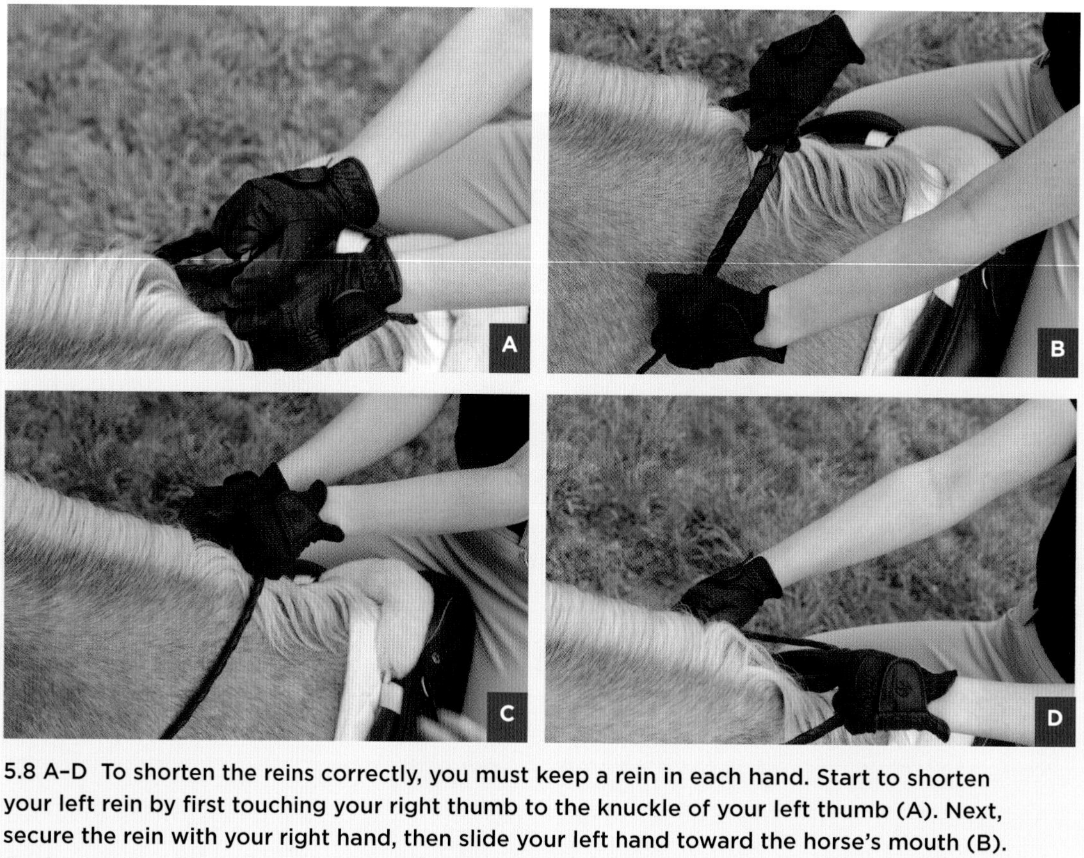

5.8 A–D To shorten the reins correctly, you must keep a rein in each hand. Start to shorten your left rein by first touching your right thumb to the knuckle of your left thumb (A). Next, secure the rein with your right hand, then slide your left hand toward the horse's mouth (B). To shorten the right rein, touch your left thumb to the knuckle of your right thumb and close the left index finger around the rein (C). Finish by holding the right rein in your left hand and sliding your right hand toward the horse's mouth (D).

THE WRIST MAGIC BAND

The *Wrist Magic Band* is one of my most versatile Teaching Tools, and it can be used on its own or in combination with the *Elbow Magic Band*. I use the *Wrist Magic Band* to help correct a myriad of wrist-position problems, but also for riders that see-saw on the reins, those who have one hand that always comes higher than the other, and those still working toward independence of the arms and torso.

To make your own *Wrist Magic Band,* there are two options. For Option A, use the same 1-inch-wide stretchy elastic you used to create your *Elbow Magic Band*. Cut the elastic about 18 inches long, fold it in half so the ends meet, and tie them together in a basic knot. Slide the *Band* around your wrists; it should be tight enough that when the wrists are held in the riding position, they are about 6 inches apart when all slack is taken out of the *Band* (fig. 5.9 A).

Option B is to purchase an elastic sports-style headband, ideally less than half an inch wide. These come already sewn in a circular band, so you will not need to tie any knots in them (fig. 5.9 B).

Just like with the *Elbow Magic Band,* if a rider gets in trouble and needs more mobility in her arms, the *Wrist Magic Band* will easily slide off over the back of her hand toward her fingers (fig. 5.9 C).

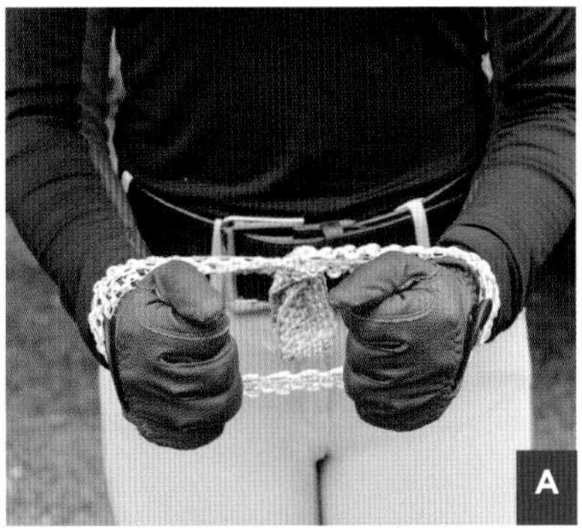

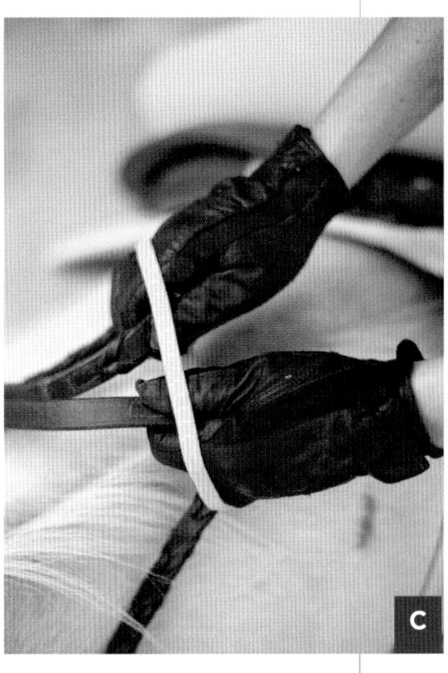

5.9 A–C You can make your *Wrist Magic Band* by tying an 18-inch piece of stretchy elastic in a knot (A). You can also use an elastic sports-style headband and use it as a *Wrist Magic Band* (B). The *Wrist Magic Band* will easily slide off in case of emergency (C).

she just tries to shorten her reins, her horse is probably going to pull back. The horse weighs at least 1,000 pounds, and the rider may weigh 150 pounds. How can she possibly prevent the horse from pulling her arm straight with arm strength alone?

The rider's correct arm position starts in the shoulder, and in order to keep the shoulder blades back and the upper body stacked over the hips, the rider needs a solid core to maintain her position. A strong core is the rider's anchor, and I will talk a lot more about the core in chapter 7 (see p. 84). With a strong core holding the rider centered, a horse with

COACH SALLY'S CRAFT STICK CORRECTION

Occasionally, I will work with a rider who has such an ingrained habit of holding her wrists incorrectly that *Wrist Magic Bands* just don't make the correction stick. For these riders, I pull out the "big guns"—a set of half-inch-wide craft sticks from my local fabric store (fig. 5.10 A).

Craft sticks are made of a sturdy but thin wood, similar to a tongue depressor from the doctor's office. They are firm enough to give a rider a strong correction if she pops her wrist out of position but are soft enough to not cause harm or injury if something goes wrong.

You will need to wear a pair of gloves to use Coach Sally's *Craft Stick Correction*. Slide the craft stick inside the glove on the palm side of your wrist, until it meets the base of your fingers (fig. 5.10 B). The craft stick should be centered in the middle of the wrist. Any time you start to bend or break at the wrist, you will feel the pressure of the craft stick as an immediate reminder to return to the correct, slightly curved wrist position (fig. 5.10 C).

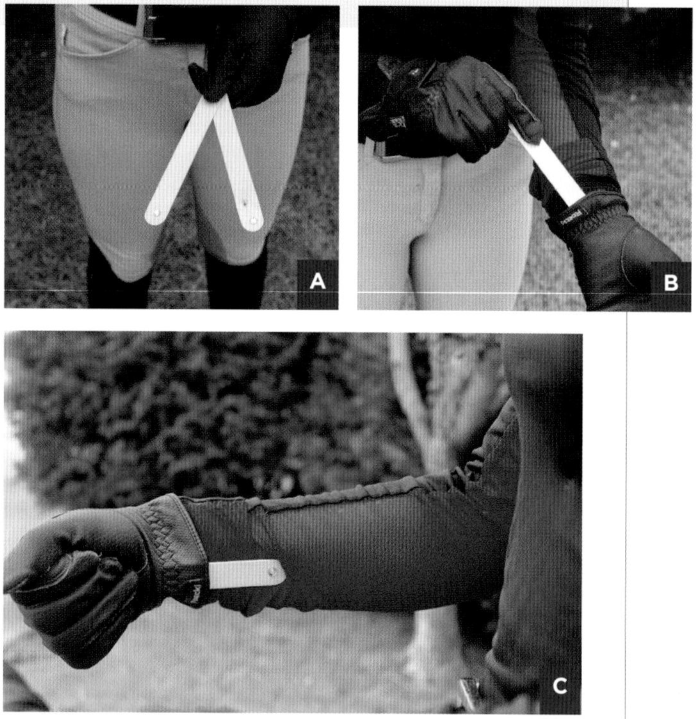

5.10 A–C Craft sticks can be used to aid the rider in keeping her wrists from breaking out or breaking in. You can add bling like this, paint them, or even purchase them in different colors to make them more fun (A)! Slide the craft stick into the palm side of your glove (B). Emmaree's correctly placed craft sticks prevent her wrists from breaking out (C).

COACH SALLY'S TOP 10 TIPS

Tip 5: Sing Your Way to Relaxation

Horses are the ultimate barometers for rider tension. Whether the rider is tightening her shoulders, gripping with her thighs or knees, or is even just holding her breath, the horse will feel it. When it comes to developing an elastic connection with the horse through a bent, following elbow, even slight tension will creep its way out of the rider through the reins to the horse's mouth. Tense riders create tense horses, and vice versa (fig. 5.11).

5.11 Hope sings out loud, releasing tension and creating a softer position.

5.12 Try playing music while you ride to reduce stress. Marin cannot help but smile during her warm up to music, which in turn relaxes her body.

When I notice that tension is beginning to impede rider effectiveness, my favorite go-to solution is quite simple—I have the rider sing. In a group lesson, I have every rider sing, which is usually more fun and prevents the tense rider from feeling singled out (which just increases her tension). The song doesn't matter—it could be the "ABC" song, or "Row, Row, Row Your Boat," or a Top 40 barn favorite, but I want to hear it loud and proud. When the rider sings, she has to breathe. When the rider keeps her breath moving, tension will leave her body with each exhale (fig. 5.12).

Sometimes, it can even be helpful to play music in the background during a warm-up or practice set. According to scientists, hearing music improves many aspects of brain function, resulting in reduced stress, improved cognitive and motor skills, and spatial-temporal learning (see https://www.ucf.edu/pegasus/your-brain-on-music/).

a low head carriage, or one that yanks on the reins or tosses his head, won't cause her to lose her position.

I have noticed that riders of naturally high-headed horses often develop a unique wrist deviation, which I call "milk maid wrists." In an attempt to get the horse to soften at the poll and lower his head and neck, these riders will alternately rotate their wrists, bringing their closed thumb forward and downward toward the saddle. When the high-headed horse is also quite energetic (as many Morgans, Saddlebreds, and other naturally high-headed breeds are), the rider may also be pulling back in an attempt to slow the tempo. The combined effect is not one of harmony or ease, but instead increased resistance from the horse and more pulling from the rider.

Riders with busy hands that seesaw the reins, riders with wrist deviations that create stiffness, riders with asymmetry who hold one hand higher than the other, as well as our milk maids on high-headed horses, are all candidates for the *Wrist Magic Band*.

Wrist Magic Bands are also helpful body awareness tools for the rider that posts with her hands. When a rider posts, the arms should stay still. The upper body should come forward, almost through the upper arms, and her engaged core helps to support this movement. But a lot of riders post with their arms and torso as one solid unit, meaning that their hands post up and down along with their upper body.

The *Wrist Magic Band* serves as a subconscious cue and visual aid for the rider. She can feel it on the outer wrist of both hands, and this tactile sensation serves as a reminder to keep the hands low and quiet. At the same time, *Wrist Magic Bands* remind riders to maintain a correct wrist alignment, and when they forget or revert to bad habits, the *Band* will immediately slide out of place.

6

Flat-Back Roll-Ups and Eyes-Up Goggles:

Improving Upper Body Posture

Riding in balance with the horse is all about alignment—the rider is responsible for centering her body over the horse's center of gravity at all gaits on the flat and during all phases of the jumping effort. A rider in correctly maintained alignment is supporting the horse rather than impeding his forward motion and impulsion (fig. 6.1).

6.1 A rider in correctly maintained alignment will be supporting the horse rather than impeding him. The rider is responsible for centering her body over the horse's center of gravity at all gaits on the flat and during all phases of the jumping effort.

In my experience, learning to feel correct upper body posture is one of the hardest concepts for a rider to master if she doesn't have someone watching her all the time. Rounded, slumped, or rolled-over shoulders are among the most common equitation faults, yet most riders have no idea they are holding their bodies incorrectly (fig. 6.2). In particular, many riders lose their upper body alignment completely in both upward and downward transitions. Unfortunately, correct posture is simply one of the hardest qualities for riders to feel on

6.2 Jinae's shoulders are slumped and rolled forward, which is negatively impacting her upper-body position.

6.3 Most of us spend time each day slumped over our computers, which can lead to rounded shoulders on the horse.

the horse. Until correct posture becomes your habit, you will need to concentrate on improving your posture every time you ride.

Most of us didn't attend etiquette classes growing up, where we would have learned to sit and walk elegantly with a perfectly straight back. In addition, we spend an ever-increasing amount of time at a desk or working over a computer, which can encourage rounded shoulders if you don't choose to hold them differently (fig. 6.3). The fact is that many riders climb into the saddle almost primed to ride with their shoulders slumped. This incorrect posture has immediate and significant negative impacts on the balance of both horse and rider and the effectiveness of the rider's aids.

Riding with rounded shoulders causes the rider's upper body to lean too far forward, burdening the horse's forehand. Rounded shoulders will also reduce the ability of her elastic, following elbow to maintain a soft connection with the horse's mouth. In addition, nine times out of ten, a rider with rounded shoulders will also have a dropped head. Your head weighs between eight and 10 pounds, and that is plenty of extra burden to further disrupt the horse's natural balance (fig. 6.4).

I have been riding horses most of my life and use my aids so instinctively that I can't always remember what it felt like when I was first learning. In order for me to keep my teaching skills fresh and on point, I enjoy trying new sports or activities that I've never done before.

One year, I took advantage of free rowing lessons from the Dartmouth Outing Club. In order to row my single scull boat effectively, I was to round my back all the way forward, then lie all the way back as I pulled on the oars. I thought I was doing a pretty good job but my boat wasn't making much progress. My coach kept telling me that I had to round my back over; I felt that I couldn't possibly round it any more than I was already doing. As it turns out, my lifelong practice of maintaining correct upper body posture for riding made it incredibly difficult for me to round my shoulders and spine forward, even on purpose (fig. 6.5)!

I share this specific experience with you because it brings up several important principles. First, it reminds me how hard it is to learn a new skill or movement, and motivated riders of all levels are learning new skills and movements nearly every lesson. Secondly, despite our best efforts, habits from other aspects of our lives will impact us as we are trying to learn these new skills and movements. Finally, it is yet another example of how our own perception of what our bodies are doing may not match what is actually happening; developing body

6.4 Rayelle practices walking with a book on her head to learn to balance without looking down.

6.5 Try new sports and activities to increase your body awareness.

6.6 Claire developed her body awareness through repetition so that she would have the correct upper-body alignment in competition. Developing body awareness of how it feels to execute movements correctly is key to being able to repeat them both in practice and in competition.

awareness of how it feels to execute a movement correctly is key to being able to repeat it (fig. 6.6).

Learning to ride with correct upper body posture means that the rider has chosen to practice a different habit, one where she is able to keep her shoulders stacked over her hips. To help install this kinesthetic awareness, I use one of my Teaching Tools: *Flat-Back Roll-Ups* (see sidebar).

Exercise: Using Flat-Back Roll-Ups for Posture Correction

Place one *Flat-Back Roll-Up* under each armpit, centering it so that about the same amount of *Roll-Up* protrudes on each side of your shoulder. Position the *Roll-Up* so that the front end is angled slightly upward, about 30 degrees. In order to maintain the *Roll-Up* in this position, you will need to engage the muscles of the upper back, which will pull your shoulders

MAKING FLAT-BACK ROLL-UPS

Flat-Back Roll-Ups are another of my easy-to-make-at-home Teaching Tools to add to your riding bag. For riders with an ingrained habit of riding with rounded shoulders, I use *Flat-Back Roll-Ups* for 10 minutes at all gaits, then take them away to see if the new posture can be maintained. These are easy to use on your own, as well, because you can see them out of the corner of your eye while you are riding and can readily prop them on the edge of the arena when not in use (fig. 6.7 A).

To make your *Roll-Ups*, you will need two slender magazines that are stapled, not bound, and about 8 by 11 inches. I like to use the kinds of magazines that you might impulse-buy at the grocery store checkout—they are the right size, weight, and malleability (fig. 6.7 B). You will also need a roll of sturdy packing tape. Precut several pieces of tape, about 6 inches in length, and have them handy.

Starting at the binding side of the magazine, roll it up as tightly as you can. The tightness of the roll is critical to its usefulness; if it is not tight, the strength of your biceps will make the *Roll-Up* collapse and become ineffective (fig. 6.7 C). When you are done, the *Roll-Up* should be so tight that there is almost no light visible through the tube. Without releasing the roll, take one of your precut pieces of tape and wrap it around the middle of the *Roll-Up* to secure it (fig. 6.7 D). Then move on to each of the ends, and, finally, use your remaining tape to cover the whole *Roll-Up* completely. This step is critical, as it makes your *Roll-Up* sweat and water-resistant (fig. 6.7 E).

If you get the *Roll-Up* tight enough and thoroughly wrap it in tape, I find that it holds up quite well to repeated arena use, even under hot conditions.

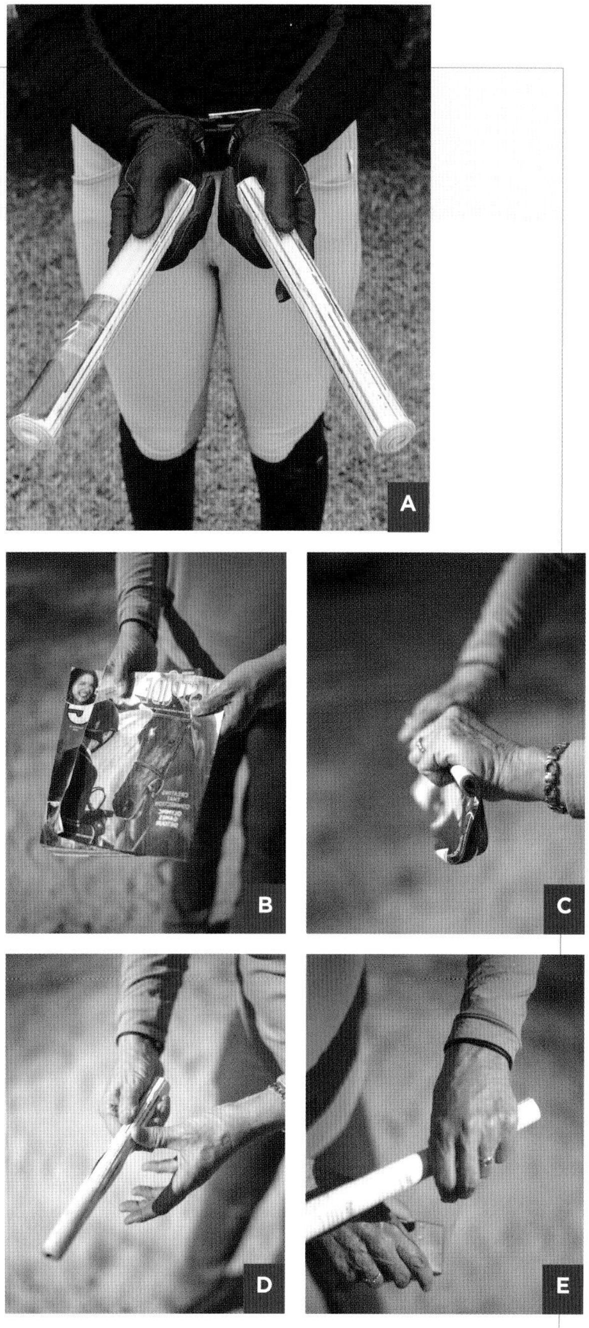

6.7 A–E *Flat-Back Roll-Ups* can help a rider improve her posture (A). To make your *Flat-Back Roll-Ups*, find two slender magazines (B). Start the roll from the stapled side of the magazine and roll it tightly (C). Place tape around both ends of your *Flat-Back Roll-Up* (D). Wrap the tape around the entire *Flat-Back Roll-Up* to secure the magazine from unrolling (E).

6.8 A & B Correct placement of *Flat-Back Roll-Ups* under Jerianne's armpits and pointed up in the front (A). When you stop using your upper back muscles to secure the *Flat Back Roll-Ups*, they will drop down to your elbows (B).

back, down, and into correct alignment (fig. 6.8 A).

Start at the walk, until you get used to the feeling of the *Roll-Ups*, then move on to the trot and canter. Usually, riders can monitor the angled end of the *Roll-Up* from the corners of their eyes, ensuring that their upper bodies are maintaining the correct position. But not to worry—if you stop using the upper back muscles to support your correct shoulder posture, your *Roll-Ups* will start to slide down the arm until they fall out or you are holding them with your elbows. When this happens, stop, reset, then get back to practicing (fig. 6.8 B).

KEEP YOUR HEAD UP

I mentioned earlier that many riders with rounded shoulders also drop their head forward; sometimes, even when we correct the upper body posture, this old habit remains. As instructors, we can remind a rider over and over to look up, but most of the time when she begins to concentrate on something else, her eyes will simply resume their usual, familiar downward gaze. But if a rider wants to execute smooth, effortless transitions and ensure invisible communication with her horse on the flat and over fences, breaking the bad habit

6.9 A & B If Stella stays balanced on Swazi's back, Swazi can stay upright and carry her (A). If Stella leans forward, her weight pushes Swazi forward and she needs to take steps to regain her balance (B).

of dropping her head and looking down is essential.

If you have ever given a child or friend a piggyback ride or carried them on your shoulders, you know firsthand how disruptive that extra, mobile weight is to your balance. In order to stay upright with this burden, you must keep your head up and stack your shoulders over your hips (fig. 6.9 A). If your "rider" tips forward, you immediately scramble to keep your collective balance or risk falling (fig. 6.9 B).

Horses are rear-wheel-drive: Their power is in their hindquarters, and they need to do both upward and downward transitions from the hind end first. When the rider habitually looks down, it has the effect of causing the horse to run on his forehand. With extra weight on the forehand (and the horse naturally already carries as much as 60 percent of his weight there), rear-wheel-drive transitions are not possible. The horse, figuratively, just spins his wheels.

My number one Teaching Tool to help riders break their old habit of looking down are *Eyes-Up Goggles* (see sidebar).

EYES-UP GOGGLES

Eyes-Up Goggles are one Teaching Tool that you will not have to make! Visit your local sporting goods or department store (or order online), and look for "basketball dribbling glasses." These specialized sport glasses are usually black, made of soft rubber with an adjustable strap, and sold singly or in packs. The bottom half of the "glasses" is blacked out with a half-moon of rubber. The wearer can still see, but if she looks down, all she sees is the black rubber. The best part is they are not expensive; I usually spend less than $5 on a pair (fig. 6.10 A). Unfortunately, *Eyes-Up Goggles* don't work great over eyeglasses, as the latter will fog up.

When a rider habitually looks down, she is usually not aware she is doing so. But when she wears *Eyes-Up Goggles*, she is reminded—immediately—when her eyes leave their designated focal point out ahead of her. *Eyes-Up Goggles* are also useful for a rider learning to feel for her posting diagonals and canter leads, because if she tries to confirm them visually, all she will see is the black rubber.

When putting them on, many riders try to pull the goggles over their helmets, which never works. To put your *Eyes-Up Goggles* on effectively, try this:

1. Bring your horse to the halt. If he doesn't stand perfectly still, have a friend hold him.

6.10 A–D *Eyes-Up Goggles* are used to keep the rider's eyes up, and can also be used to help riders learn their posting diagonals and canter leads by feel (A). To put on the *Eyes-Up Goggles*, hold the goggles to the face and pull the strap up and over your helmet brim (B). Correct placement of the *Eyes-Up Goggles* over the eyes and the strap over the helmet crown (C). If you place the strap straight back, it will fall off the helmet. After wearing *Eyes-Up Goggles* for about 15 minutes, pull them down around the neck and practice keeping your eyes up (D).

2. Lift the *Goggles* toward your eyes, half-moon side on the bottom, while lifting the elastic strap over your helmet visor (fig. 6.10 B).

3. Hold the bridge of the *Goggles* in place over your nose, and slide the strap toward the crown of your helmet.

4. Continue to slide the *Goggle* strap until it is just past the crown of your helmet. Do not pull it all the way around the back, as it tends to slide down (fig. 6.10 C).

I have riders use *Eyes-Up Goggles* for about 15 minutes, then pull the *Goggles* down and wear them like a necklace while they practice maintaining the feeling. This way, the *Goggles* are readily available to put back in place when needed (fig. 6.10 D).

Eyes-Up Goggles pair perfectly with *Flat-Back Roll-Ups* for the ultimate correction of both upper body posture and head/eye position (fig. 6.11)!

6.11 *Eyes-Up Goggles* can be paired with *Flat-Back Roll-Ups* for the ultimate strong upper body posture.

TESTING YOUR POSTURE PRACTICE WITH THE TROT-CANTER TRANSITION

Now that you have practiced your correct upper body posture enough to make it a habit, it is time for the "final exam"—maintaining upper body alignment during an upward transition to canter. This transition is a show ring essential, and executing it correctly will quickly help riders move to the top of a judge's card. Before I begin, let's review the horse's biomechanics in an upward transition to better understand why the rider's alignment is so critical.

Regardless of whether you are asking from the walk or the trot, smooth and balanced canter transitions are the result of the rider's correctly applied, clear aids. In both the walk

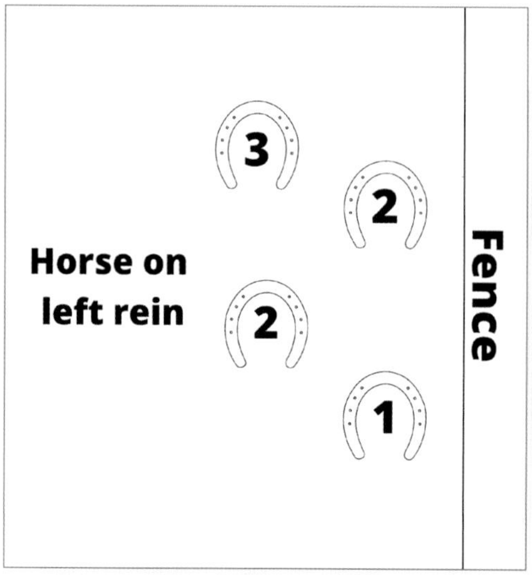

6.12 The correct sequence of footfalls for the left lead canter: outside right hind, diagonal pair, and then inside left front.

6.13 A & B The rider's leg is too far back for a right lead canter cue (A). The lower leg is behind the "Go" button and could irritate the horse. Now the rider's left leg is slightly back, in the correct position to ask for a right lead canter (B).

and trot, there is only one moment during each stride at which the horse is biomechanically capable of picking up the inside lead of the canter. Therefore, to be effective, riders need to not only know that the walk has four beats, the trot two, and the canter three, but the sequence of the footfalls in each gait.

In all my years of coaching, I would estimate that as many as 90 percent of the riders I worked with did not know the correct sequence of the canter footfalls. Most assumed that the inside front leg strikes the first canter beat, which is perhaps a reasonable guess since that is the leg we check for the lead. But the canter actually starts with the outside hind leg, followed by the diagonal pair, then the leading inside fore, followed by a moment of suspension. Remember, the horse is rear-wheel-drive, and we cue the canter with our outside leg because we are trying to influence the action of the horse's outside hind leg (fig. 6.12).

It is pretty common to see riders draw their outside leg way too far back when asking for the canter depart (fig. 6.13 A). Some horses mistake this as a request to yield their haunches sideways, while others find the leg irritating, even kicking out or crow-hopping in response. Others simply ignore the mis-positioned aid altogether. Ideally, when asking for the canter, the rider should draw her leg only three to six inches back from her normal, passive leg position (fig. 6.13 B).

To see if you are guilty of bringing your outside leg too far back, halt your horse parallel to an arena mirror, then, without looking, instinctively draw your leg back into its canter depart position and hold it there. Without moving, glance to the mirror to see if your lower leg is within the acceptable 3- to 6-inch range, or if you have committed the crime of drawing the leg up or back more than needed. No mirrors? Ask a friend to snap a photo on her phone and show you the image right away, while the kinesthetic memory is still fresh.

6.14 Jinae is checking her horse's left lead by looking down with just her eyes, not her whole head.

Riders must keep their eyes up throughout the entire transition to canter. Once the horse is cantering, some riders will need to use their eyes to check the horse's canter lead. Do not let your whole head drop if you do this—look just with your eyes, seeking the inside shoulder or tip of the inside hoof (fig. 6.14). Most horses feel pretty awkward when they are on the wrong (outside) lead, and usually once a rider becomes familiar with the smoother feeling of the correct

6.15 Sherry is in perfect harmony with her horse at the canter.

(inside) lead, she finds she no longer needs to visually confirm the lead after a transition.

Exercise: Trot-to-Canter Transition Position Check

Today, you will be using your transition to canter as a position check to see if your correct posture practice has given you the strength and stability to maintain correct alignment. Different horses have different skillsets, so if you typically ask for the canter out of the trot, this is the transition to start with. The ultimate goal, however, is to develop correctly balanced transitions from walk to canter, particularly if competition is in your future (fig. 6.15).

To ask for a correct canter transition from the trot:

1. Establish a positive forward posting trot with 5 pounds of contact in each hand.
2. Mentally review the correct canter aids: a slight inside direct rein, an outside supporting rein, inside leg in its normal, slightly behind-the-girth position, outside leg not more than 6 inches back.
3. Roll your weight onto the inside ball of each foot to keep your weight down into the stirrup, and check to make sure your shoulders are still stacked over your hips.

6.16 Amanda's upper body is too far forward for a canter transition and she has also dropped her eyes and head.

6.17 Amanda has corrected her canter-transition position by putting on her *Eyes-Up Goggles* and *Flat-Back Roll-Ups.*

4. Sit the trot, half-halt, and apply the canter aid with your outside leg.

At this point, one of two things will happen—your horse will canter, or he will not. If he canters, congratulations! You have maintained your correct upper body posture and effectively cued the transition. But don't make the common mistake of celebrating the canter transition by taking your outside leg off and moving it back into its neutral position, as this is actually part of the cue for a downward transition back to trot. Instead, keep the outside leg in its canter cue position, and reapply the aid as needed. Also be sure to keep your eyes focused up and forward, and maintain your upper-body posture.

If your horse did not canter, or cantered but on the wrong lead, you need to assess what went wrong. The most common mistake I see is that the rider brings her upper body too far forward in the transition, or worse, collapses her shoulders and head forward over the pommel (fig. 6.16). If this happens to you, try riding the transition again with the *Flat-Back Roll-Ups* and/or *Eyes-Up Goggles* in place. Pay close attention to the changes these Tools cause in your posture and focus. Practice several transitions, then take the Tools away and see if you can maintain the correction (fig. 6.17).

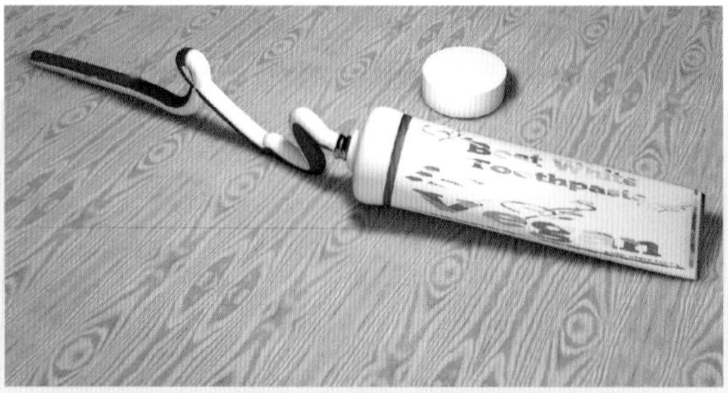

6.18 When a rider asks for the canter transition without the correct rein length, it is like squeezing a tube of toothpaste with the cap off: all the energy goes out the front.

The next most common mistake I see is the rider allowing her reins to get too long. For a horse to be correctly balanced on his haunches in the canter depart, the rider needs 5 pounds of pressure on each rein, or even as much as 8 pounds if the horse is quite downhill.

Imagine that your horse is like a tube of toothpaste, and your reins are the cap. We all know what happens if we give a hard squeeze to an open toothpaste tube (fig. 6.18). If we squeeze our horse with both legs but do not provide him with enough support in the reins, all of that energy will shoot forward, putting the horse onto his forehand.

When riders make this canter transition mistake, the horse usually responds by power trotting around the ring. He may eventually pick up the canter just because he gets tired of the rider's kicking legs, but the transition is anything but harmonious and the resulting canter far from balanced (fig. 6.19 A).

6.19 A–C Rebecca's reins are too long for the canter transition (B). Usually, this will cause the horse to fall on his forehand and just power trot around the arena instead of canter. Rebecca can help her horse get an inside bend by slightly lifting her inside hand for the canter transition (B). Here she lifts her inside hand too high for the canter transition (C).

Finally, some riders allow the horse to bend to the outside during the transition, essentially setting him up for the wrong lead. It is the rider's job to maintain a slight inside bend when asking for the canter. She can further support the request for the inside position by slightly lifting the inside hand during the depart—just a little, so as to be hardly visible (figs. 6.19 B & C).

This is also one of my favorite techniques to use at collegiate horse shows where riders are mounted on unfamiliar horses. If one of my riders drew a horse who we observed had a sticky lead in warm-ups, I coached them to lift the inside rein with enough pressure that the horse's head was lifted to the inside and the rider could see his inside eye. In addition, both

COACH SALLY'S TOP 10 TIPS

Tip 6: Be Assertive, Not Aggressive

When it comes to riding effectively, nine-tenths of the challenge is convincing the horse that the rider is in charge. This important concept will affect everything you do with your horse, from leading him safely to jumping a course to enjoying a trail ride with friends. Being a competent leader for the horse requires assertive aids from the rider, and the horse must understand that his job is to answer her promptly.

When I say "be assertive," I do not mean that we want to be aggressive, or excessively use our natural or artificial aids, or apply strong gadgets for control. I'm not talking about roughly handling the horse or being cruel. *Being assertive* means that the rider has confidence in her aids and what she is asking of the horse, and the horse is left with no question in his mind regarding what the rider is asking, or that he must answer (fig. 6.20).

6.20 Meg is confident and assertive in a collegiate competition over fences.

Many people I teach are not assertive in their regular lives, and it is extremely difficult for them to be assertive on a horse. But when a rider asks too quietly or tentatively with her aids, the horse usually will ignore her. As a coach, it becomes my responsibility to ensure that riders know the proper steps for every transition or movement, and that they are doing it the right way, every time.

of the rider's legs should be driving the horse forward. The rider should maintain a minimum of 5 pounds of pressure in each hand throughout the transition—don't throw the outside rein away.

Once you have done some troubleshooting on any problematic transitions, go out to the rail and practice a series of five trot-canter-trot transitions, using a visual like an arena letter or fence post as a marker for the change of gait. As you approach the marker, go through the checklist for the canter transition (see p. 74), then apply your canter cue at the marker itself. Another option is to practice the transitions on a 20-meter circle or in the corners, which naturally puts the rider's aids (and horse's body) in the correct place for the inside lead (fig. 6.21).

6.21 Rebecca asks for the right lead canter as she bends her horse around a circle, which naturally puts her aids in the correct places.

Exercise: Canter-to-Trot Transition Position Check

When preparing for the *downward* transition from canter to trot, first bring the outside leg back toward the girth, to its neutral position. Maintain the upper body alignment, with eyes up and shoulders opened and stacked over the hips. Squeeze the reins like a sponge, and the horse should softly come back to the trot.

Many riders end up working too hard to get the correct posting diagonal after the downward transition to the trot. If your horse was on the correct canter lead, rise with the first trot stride after the downward transition (while keeping your eyes up), and you will always be posting on the correct diagonal (fig.

6.22 Rebecca rises on her horse's first trot stride after a correct lead canter, which will always put her onto the correct diagonal.

6.22). Many riders have gotten into the (bad) habit of looking for their diagonal, especially after the canter, and this is totally not necessary. *Eyes-Up Goggles* can help break this habit.

TYING IT TOGETHER: THE WALK-TO-CANTER TRANSITION

Getting ready to do walk-canter transitions is a perfect opportunity to practice being assertive. This transition is simply not possible without an active, marching walk, and it is the rider's job to create this energy by assertively using alternating leg pressure—here's how:

Exercise: Get a Marching Walk

Start in your horse's "normal" walk, which for most animals is usually not much more than a casual stroll. Relax your seat and allow your hips and back to passively follow the horse. Next, bring your mental focus to the movement of your right hip. When the horse's right hind pushes forward, the rider's right hip will swing through in time with the horse. Once you can feel how your hips follow the motion of the horse, it is time to add some leg (fig. 6.23).

When the horse's barrel fills your right leg, and you feel your hip swing, take your leg from

6.23 Simone F. does her alternating leg at the walk by applying her left leg as her horse's right leg steps forward.

passive to active for that beat of the walk, then release. Now you will feel the horse's barrel fill your left leg while your left hip swings; activate your left leg for that beat, then release. Continue alternating passive and active contact with each leg until the horse's walk transforms into one with marching, positive energy.

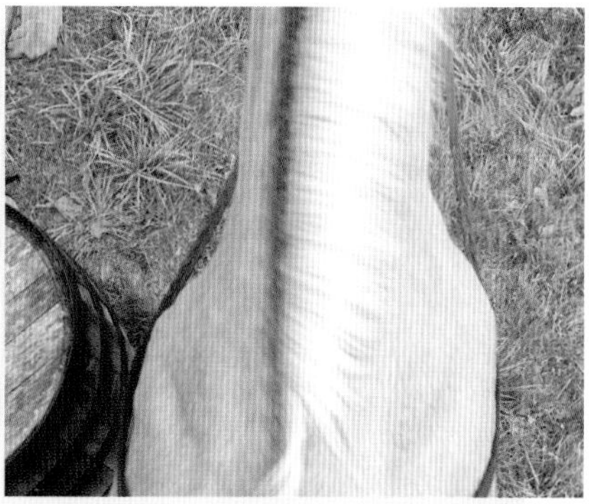

6.24 As the rider looks down at the horse's shoulders, she can see that the right shoulder is ahead of the left shoulder and so she will increase the pressure of her left leg.

If you struggle to match the feeling of the horse's movement with the movement of your hips, try this approach instead. When the horse's inside shoulder goes forward (look with your eyes without dropping your head), close the outside leg, then release (fig. 6.24). In the next beat, the outside shoulder will swing forward, and you will close the inside leg, then release. Continue this alternating pattern, closing your left leg when the horse's right shoulder goes forward, then the right leg when his left shoulder goes forward.

As with anything involving animals, there are always a few exceptions. I would not recommend using the alternating leg aid on a games or barrel horse, or any animal that only understands the leg to mean GO. But most pleasure or lesson horses will understand the alternating leg cue and will respond by simply marching more forward. It is always amazing to watch the horse transform from moving in a lazy gait to one that makes him look like he is late for his next meal (fig. 6.25 A). The horse's eyes brighten and he begins to take more interest in his work. From now on, forever more, you are going to assertively use your alternating legs at the walk, right from the first few steps away from the mounting block (fig. 6.25 B). This simple aid shows the horse, from the very beginning of the day's work, that his rider expects him to pay attention to her and to stay forward-thinking.

6.25 A & B Simone F's horse is sluggish and sleepy at the walk (A). She applies her alternating leg and her horse marches brightly forward (B). She could improve her horse's walk even more by shortening her reins and increasing the contact.

Exercise: Create a Level Balance

Riding correct and balanced canter transitions is all about perseverance. Once you have mastered the transition from trot to canter, it is time to try the harder option—walk to canter. Before riders try a walk-canter transition, it is important to make sure that the horse is off his forehand and working toward level balance. To help create this balance, I like to use a series of prompt trot-walk-trot transitions, or even trot-halt-trot, with the rider actively engaging her deep seat in the saddle. In chapter 7, I will discuss the rider's seat and its use in transitions in much more detail (see p. 84).

Exercise: Walk-Canter Transition

After you have done a series of five to seven trot-walk-trot or trot-halt-trot transitions to bring your horse to a level balance, return to the walk. Using alternating leg pressure, encourage the horse to march actively forward. Allow your seat to follow the horse's swinging back, and check that you are still keeping your shoulders stacked over your hips. Choose an arena marker out ahead of you at which to do the transition.

As you approach the arena marker, go through your canter transition steps in your head. At the marker, apply the canter aids exactly as you did in the transition from trot: maintain inside bend with about 5 pounds of pressure in each rein, inside leg in its usual position just at the girth, and outside leg

6.26 If your horse is not listening to your leg cue, you can try lifting the outside heel up slightly to increase the pressure for the canter transition.

6.27 If your horse is not listening to your leg aid for the canter, you can supplement your leg aid by applying the crop right behind it.

drawn back not more than 6 inches. Use your legs assertively to cue the canter; at first, some horses will require slightly more pressure from the outside leg when doing the transition out of the walk.

Did it work? If not, don't be discouraged. Instead, analyze what you felt in your body during the failed attempt in order to correct it.

A common mistake is when the horse moves to trot rather than canter. This is usually the result of the rider letting her reins get too long—the equivalent of taking the cap off the toothpaste—and the energy created from her assertive legs simply propels the horse forward. To prevent this mistake, shorten your reins, keep your fingers closed so that you are touching fingertips to palms, and make sure you feel steady pressure on the reins all the way through the transition.

If the horse just keeps walking, then you need to apply your leg aids more assertively. Instead of squeezing the calf to apply the canter cue, try lifting the heel up slightly until the horse can feel the inside edge of the boot, and apply the aid again (fig. 6.26).

If this still doesn't work, and you are carrying a crop, it is time to reinforce the horse's response to the rider's leg with this artificial aid. Put the reins into your inside hand and give the horse a swift tap with the crop where the leg is going to be applied—not more than 6 inches behind the girth. Remember that the crop is used to supplement the rider's leg aid and should be used where the leg is used (fig. 6.27). Do not use the crop to tap the horse on the shoulder, or on the hip (in fact, this is a great way to get bucked off). Once you have given the crop correction, put the outside hand back on the rein and immediately ask for the canter from the leg. You will now achieve the walk-canter transition.

7

Improving Seat Awareness

Through Downward Transitions

When I teach a clinic or work with new riders, one of the first things I do is ask them to show me their normal warm-up. In particular, I want to see how they use their body and aids during transitions between gaits, particularly the downward transitions. Are they holding their body tall (see chapter 6, p. 64)? Are they using their seat correctly, or are they pressing down too hard and stiffening instead?

Unfortunately, what I see most often are riders who just pull on the reins when they want the horse to slow down, and the horse either ignores the aid or becomes inverted in his back and neck (fig. 7.1). Only when a rider uses the correct aids, in the correct sequence, can she expect the horse to respond correctly as well. Ultimately, this requires demystifying the movement of the rider's seat—and that requires understanding how the horse's body affects the seat in each phase of the stride in each gait.

Back when you first learned how to ride, your instructor probably kept the aids really straightforward: the legs make the horse go and the hands make him stop. In the beginning, this is probably the easiest way to help riders develop control of the horse, but more advanced riders come to understand that riding smooth and balanced transitions is much more complex. Downward transitions, in particular, require coordination of the aids and full use of the rider's body.

Learning how to put all the pieces together requires dedicated practice and a clear understanding of how the movement of the horse influences the movement of the rider. Unfortunately, some riders never have the opportunity to learn these fundamentals, which can lead to frustration and frequent miscommunication between horse and rider. In this chapter, I will break down what good riders with a following seat do automatically during their downward transitions into a step-by-step process. Any rider can practice this on her own once she understands the required components.

THE RIDER'S PELVIS: LETTING THE RHYTHM MOVE YOU

The Walk

To get started, let's turn our attention to the movement of the rider's pelvis in the walk. At this gait, the rider is typically in her full seat, and most able-bodied riders feel fairly balanced and secure here. We think of the walk as the gait of rest, for both horse and rider, during which little effort is required. While this is true in the sense that we return to the walk to catch our breath or to give the horse a break, it should always be an active gait.

Further, the rider is hardly "just sitting" on the horse in the walk. Throughout every stride, micro-adjustments are made to the rider's balance by the muscles in her lower back, abdominal core, and hips, in response to the fact that the horse's active walk steps cause the rider's body to move in kind. In fact, if our bodies *didn't* make these adjustments, we would find ourselves simply sliding off the horse!

7.1 Olivia M. is stiff in her back, which has caused her horse to become inverted on the downward transition.

In the last chapter, you practiced using your alternating legs at the walk, so you know that the horse's barrel moves from side to side in conjunction with the movement of the horse's hind legs. In the walk, the horse's legs move laterally in a predictable, four-beat rhythm: outside hind, outside fore, inside hind, inside fore. The next time you are on your horse in a safe, enclosed arena, try closing your eyes for a few strides of the walk and let your body totally relax. Feel your upper body melt into your seat, then tune into the movement of your pelvis. How would you describe this movement to someone who has never ridden before (fig. 7.2)?

When I ask this question of my riders, most of the time they talk about side-to-side

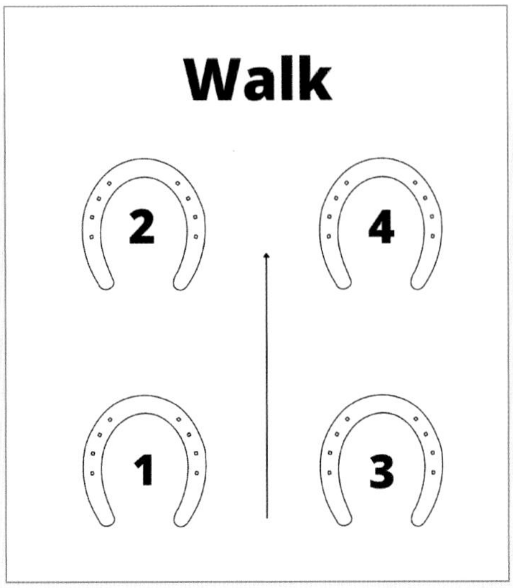

7.2 The walk is a four-beat gait with no moment of suspension, so it is generally a comfortable gait for the rider, and easy to follow.

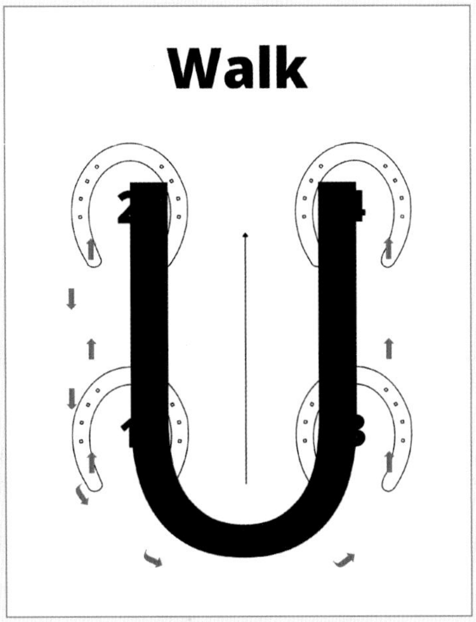

7.3 As the horse walks, the rider's pelvis needs to follow the horse's movement in a "U" shape with the open segment oriented toward the horse's ears. (The arrows indicate the direction of the seat's motion.)

movement, or forward-and-back, but neither of these descriptions is wholly accurate. Eventually, after many hints from me, they will arrive at a more correct description—the rider's pelvis moves both forward *and* sideways in each stride. Some riders describe feeling the movement like a flattened figure eight, as if a bowtie were laid across the horse's withers. If we took a bird's eye view of the rider, we could see her pelvis moves in a "U" pattern, with the open segment oriented toward the horse's ears (fig. 7.3).

Let's break down the movement of the rider's pelvis even further. As the horse's right hind steps underneath his body, the motion lifts the right side of the rider's pelvis. At the top of the stride, when the right hind is extended fully forward, the rider's right seat bone starts coming down. As the horse draws his body forward, the energy of his movement goes through the backside of the rider's pelvis, through the tailbone, to the left seat bone, and the process repeats itself on the other side. Now, the horse's left hind leg steps through and the rider's left hip tips up and in; as the horse's limb begins to push off the ground, the rider's pelvis drops back down.

In able-bodied riders, this movement happens naturally, without conscious action, because the *horse is moving the rider*. So long as the rider remains relaxed in her body, maintaining enough positive tension to hold her position, her pelvis should continue to swing easily in time with the horse's movement. Becoming effective with the seat aids first requires that the rider become aware of this passive movement in her body, and second, that she learn to control it. When a rider can choose whether to follow or influence the horse's natural movement by controlling the following action of her hips, we say that she has developed an *independent seat.*

THE RIDER'S PELVIS AS AN INFLUENCER

Now let's try experimenting with using the movement of the rider's pelvis as a tool to influence the horse's walk. Within each of the horse's basic gaits (walk, trot, and canter), there are specific variations called paces (working, shortened, lengthened). A horse that is moving in a positive forward manner, with steady level balance and acceptance of a light contact, is usually in the working variation of the gait. The working gaits are your baseline. From here, you can learn to shorten or lengthen the stride.

Influencing the Walk

Exercise: Establish the Working Walk

Ask your horse to walk along the rail and check in with your position. Make sure that you are maintaining perfect posture while applying your alternating legs and continuing to allow the seat and elastic elbow to follow the movement of your horse's back and neck. *Working walk* is business-like and purposeful, and the horse's hind foot should step into the print left by the front foot on the same side; this is called "tracking up."

Once you believe that your horse is in working walk, have a friend video several strides. When reviewing the video, keep a close watch on the horse's inside front leg. Watch where that foot lands, not letting your eye follow the leg as it continues forward. Now watch where the hind foot on the same side lands. Does the horse step into the print left by the forelimb? If so, you have achieved working walk. Memorize this feeling—it will now be your job as the rider to create the working walk in every ride.

Another option to confirm that your horse is in working walk is to rake a path between 3 and 4 feet wide and several strides long on the quarterline of the arena (fig. 7.4). Establish

7.4 I rake a path about 3 to 4 feet wide to test the horse's working, shortened, and lengthened strides.

BALANCED SEAT DISGUISED AS EQUITATION

Equitation is the dominant form of collegiate equestrian competition. Essentially, riders are scored on the correctness and effect of their position on a horse. But riders come to collegiate equestrian programs from a broad range of different backgrounds and with unique skillsets. In my program, at any given time, I have coached everyone from successful Medal/Maclay riders, to those who competed on local schooling circuits, to backyard riders, right down to rank beginners (figs. 7.5–77). But I also had riders whose primary focus had been eventing, dressage, foxhunting, or even saddle seat. Trying to effectively coach such a broad range of riders challenged me to try many different approaches to find what worked best.

One theme I recognized, particularly among those riders coming strictly from the equitation ranks, was a basic lack of understanding of how the rider's seat can positively influence the horse and encourage better performance from him. Equitation riders who are able to apply invisible aids are usually rewarded in the show ring, but many times riders entered my program using big, obvious rein aids to slow the horse, and awkward, incorrect leg cues to send him forward, usually with a tense seat.

Not surprisingly, the horse's natural response to any of these tactless aids is to resist. These riders needed to learn how their seat moved on the horse, and when and how to use it as a communication tool, all while maintaining the appearance of the

7.5 Olivia C. came to Dartmouth College with an extensive riding resume, including winning the 2013 USEF Show Jumping Talent Search West.

7.6 Elle was a casual, recreational rider before coming to Dartmouth and making the varsity team.

forward seat preferred by judges. I called my collegiate program "balanced seat disguised as equitation."

Balanced seat is a specific discipline of riding in its own right; it is most commonly associated with dressage and eventing. These riders sit more deeply in the seat, with a longer leg and more upright posture than is desirable in the equitation ring. I didn't want my collegiate riders taking their positions that far out of the forward-seat mold, but many of the essential concepts of balanced seat apply to both disciplines.

In the balanced seat, the rider's center of gravity is as close as possible to the horse's center of gravity. The rider is in correct alignment when there is a straight, vertical line from her ear to her shoulder to the point of the hip to the back of her heel. In addition, the rider's seat bones are planted in the deepest part of the saddle, with her legs underneath her (not out in front). Most importantly, a good balanced seat is relaxed and supple, not tight and tense (fig. 7.7).

By applying balanced-seat concepts, riders soon found they were able to more effectively and invisibly communicate with their horses. Our ultimate goal is to ride with invisible aids; using the seat in addition to the hands and legs not only brings the rider closer to achieving this goal, but it is also kinder to the horse. For collegiate competition, we then simply refined the rider's position so that it more closely emulated what a judge expects to see in the equitation ring, while maintaining the use of the seat.

7.7 Teaghan had only ridden Western before riding at Dartmouth, so she was considered a beginner Hunt Seat rider.

7.8 Gabby demonstrates a correct balanced-seat position, with her seat bones in the deepest part of the saddle and her seat relaxed and supple.

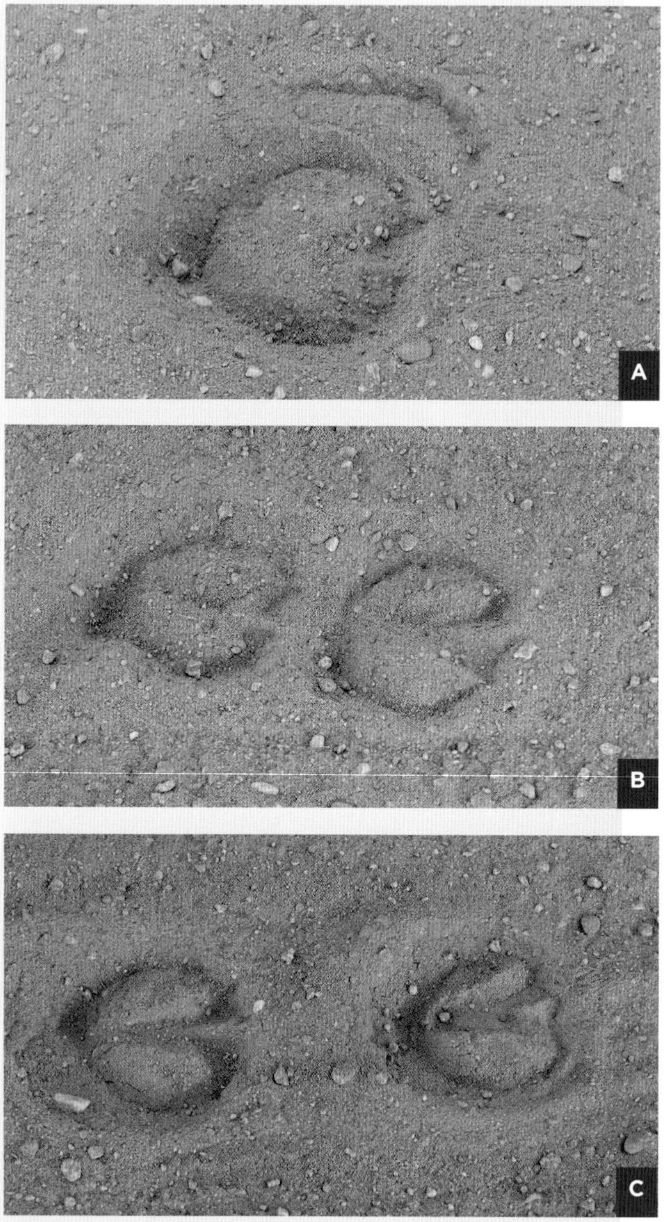

7.9 A–C In a working walk, the horse's hind foot steps into the front footprint (A). In a shortened-stride walk, the horse's hind foot steps behind the front footprint (B). In a lengthened-stride walk, the horse's hind foot steps in front of the front footprint (C).

what you believe is your horse's working walk, then ride up the raked path. Based on the hoof prints left behind, you should be able to see if the hind foot has stepped into the print of the forelimb (fig. 7.9 A). This option also tells you if the horse is stepping straight with his haunches.

Exercise: Shortening the Walk

Once you are familiar with the feeling of your horse's working walk, you are ready to try *shortening* it, using your seat as the primary aid. From the working walk, continue to use a light alternating leg aid while maintaining steady rein contact. To ask the horse to shorten stride, hold your seat still by engaging your core, particularly your middle abdominal muscles. Keep the gluteal muscles relaxed and avoid negative tension elsewhere in the body.

For some horses, this change in the rider's following seat will be enough to cue them to shorten the stride. When stilling your seat alone does not produce a sufficient response, stop the alternating leg pressure. If this is *still* not enough, close your fingers more fully around the reins, adding some resistance but not drawing the elbow back fully as you would in a downward transition to halt.

When the horse responds by correctly shortening his stride, most riders report that they feel as if the horse's hind leg is "jabbing" their seat bone as it swings forward. The horse's hind foot will land behind the print left by the foreleg on the same side (this can be quite difficult for a big-moving horse to do—fig. 7.9 B).

Usually, a rider can only maintain the shortened walk for a few strides before she loses focus and stops "holding" the horse with her seat. When this happens, release the seat fully, resume the alternating leg pressure and follow with the hips until the horse is once again in the working walk, then try shortening the stride once again. To practice this transition thoughtfully, try alternating between working walk and shortened walk using the markers around your arena as guideposts.

Exercise: Lengthening the Walk

Now you are ready to try *lengthening* the walk. To do this, your following seat is going to get as big as possible—the "U" will have long sides. While you draw out the swing of your seat, also increase the intensity of your alternating legs. Be sure to maintain the usual 5 pounds of contact in the reins, or else you will once again experience the "cap-off-the-toothpaste" effect discussed in the previous chapter (p. 76).

Without contact, the extra energy you have generated will cause the horse to fall onto his forehand and/or transition to trot. In a lengthened stride, the horse's hind foot will land in front of the print left by the foreleg on the same side; this is called "overstep" (fig. 7.9 C). When the horse is a big, elastic mover, the overstep might be more than a hoof's width, while a shorter-stepping horse may only go a tiny fraction beyond the original print. To return to the working walk, moderate the swing of your seat until it is moving in the regular sized "U," and quiet the alternating leg pressure.

Most riders are readily able to feel the mechanics of the lengthened walk and find this movement easier to create in their seat than the resistance required to shorten the gait.

Ultimately, riders with a *following seat* develop strength and control of the muscles in their core and lower back. When the seat is following, riders use both their abdominal and gluteal muscles to support their upper body. The abdominal muscles, in conjunction with the front of the hip flexors, draw the seat back, while the gluteals help to propel the seat forward. In playing with these three paces of the walk, riders are learning to better engage their core and to control their abdominals, hip flexors, and gluteal muscles. Developing this control is the foundation of a balanced seat.

Influencing the Trot

Now that you have experimented with using your seat to influence the walk, it is time to take the same concepts and apply them to the trot. Although the majority of non-dressage riders choose to post at the trot most of the time, you can still use the seat to influence the horse's way of going.

The trot is a two-beat gait, in which one diagonal pair of limbs swings forward while the other reaches back. In between beats is a moment of suspension, when all four limbs are off the ground (fig. 7.11). This is why the trot is so bouncy! The horse's conformation and breed will influence how much reach they have in the trot, and how pronounced the moment of suspension

COACH SALLY'S TOP 10 TIPS

Tip 7: (Correctly) Reward Your Horse

A successful rider-athlete knows it is important to praise her mount for his effort. Rewarding the horse is often as simple as softening the aids as soon as the horse answers or giving him a walk break on long reins after a practice round or flatwork set. But many riders are so proud of their horse's performance that they take things a step further, enthusiastically patting the horse on his neck with an open palm (fig. 7.10 A).

Whenever I see this, I cringe. We must remember that horses are intuitive, sensitive creatures that can feel tension in a rider's pinky finger. I have never met a horse that seems to enjoy being slapped on the neck for his performance, and I knew there had to be a better way for the rider to show her gratitude for his effort.

My solution? The *knuckle rub*.

To give the horse a knuckle rub reward, all the rider has to do is press her hands slightly forward until they are just in front of the withers. She then rotates her wrist and applies a gentle massaging pressure with the knuckles of her fingers along the horse's crest (fig. 7.10 B). Horses almost always respond positively to this massage, sometimes by

7.10 A & B Lexie has to take her right hand off the rein to give her horse an open-handed pat on his neck (A). Some judges penalize a rider for taking her hand off the rein in the show ring. Keeping a hand on each rein, she can easily reach down with her right hand and reward her horse with a knuckle rub (B). Lexie rides at Koko Crater Stables in Honolulu, Hawaii.

lowering their head or moving their jaw and licking their lips.

In the show ring, some judges penalize a rider for taking her hand off the rein. In a knuckle rub, the rider never takes her hand totally off the rein (as she would to give a pat), but she will release her hand from the horse's mouth for a moment—another reward for the horse. I will have a rider use the knuckle rub in a flat class after being called to line up in the center of the ring, or discreetly as she approaches the outgate after a jumping round.

Always thank and reward the horse after a ride, whether he is yours or someone else's. Show respect to him by dismounting promptly after exiting the arena, running up the stirrups, and taking the reins over his head (be sure to disconnect the rings of a running martingale from the reins). If you are a scholastic or collegiate rider, never forget that the horses you ride at shows are beloved by the horse holder and host. Thank them for providing the horse, and offer to hold him while the cooler is put back on. Never be so focused on yourself and your own performance that you forget to take care of the horse and the people around him.

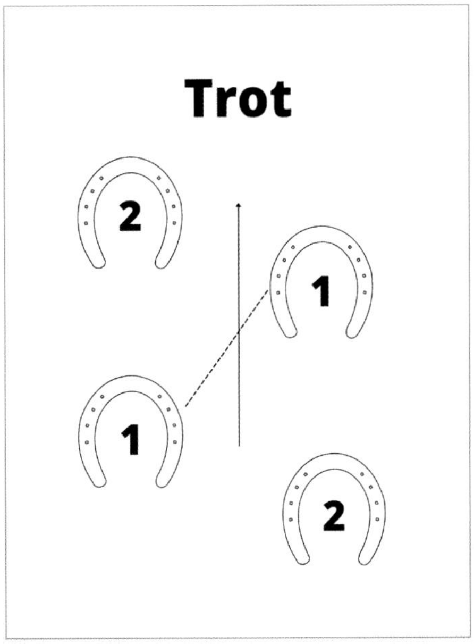

7.11 The trot is a two-beat gait with a moment of suspension with all four feet off the ground.

will be. Horses that feel smoother in the trot generally have a briefer moment of suspension.

Just as in the walk, the rider can choose to ask her horse to move in the working, shortened, or lengthened variation of the trot. Most horses have a preference, and if left to their own choice, will tend to move in their preferred variation. It is easy for riders to become complacent and allow the horse to choose how he will move in the trot, until his version of the trot feels "normal."

Exercise: Establish Working Trot

I will ask riders to show me their horse's "normal" trot, then inquire whether that trot is *working, shortened*, or *lengthened*. The criteria

7.12 Hope posts a little higher over the pommel to encourage her horse to lengthen his stride from a working trot to a lengthened trot.

for *working trot* is the same as it is for *working walk*; the horse must move positively forward, with steady level balance and soft acceptance of the contact, and the hind foot should step into the print left by the front foot in each stride. To determine if your horse's "normal" trot is also his working trot, again enlist the help of a friend to take a short video clip, or get your rake out and use the quarterline technique outlined earlier.

Most often, what a rider thinks is her horse's working trot is in fact a *shortened trot*, meaning that she will need to actively use her seat to increase the length of her horse's stride until his "normal" trot is the working variation.

To encourage a horse to move from his comfortable, shortened trot to a correct working trot, the rider will add a little extra emphasis to the "up" beat of her post. As she lifts her pelvis from the center of the saddle and brings it toward the pommel, the rider should add a few extra fractions of an inch to the arc her hips travel (fig. 7.12). In the "down" beat, squeeze both legs at the same time; this is the trotting equivalent of using the alternating legs in the walk.

If the horse is quite reluctant to increase his stride length, the rider may have to imagine that she is going to push her ankles or heels together through the horse's barrel as she squeezes in her down beat. As a rider works to learn this method of encouraging increased stride length, the most common fault is that she loses the posting rhythm, accidently standing an extra beat.

Some horses are naturally expressive, powerful movers, and comfortably take a lengthened stride as their "normal" trot. These horses need to learn to moderate their step, and their rider needs to help them to do that. To ask the horse to shorten his stride, the rider starts by keeping her post lower and closer to the saddle. If this is not enough, hold the down beat just a fraction longer, without losing the posting rhythm entirely (you don't want to sit an extra beat).

Think back to the *Equicize* series (p. 21),

CHANGING SPEED VS. CHANGING STRIDE LENGTH

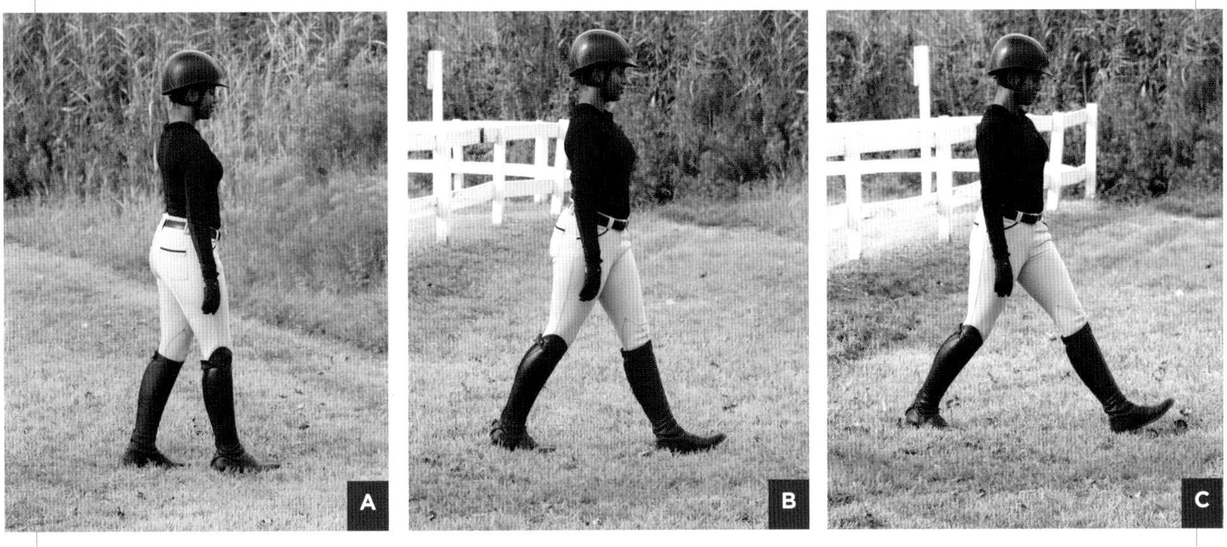

7.13 A–C Simone T. takes smaller steps to demonstrate the shortened strides of the horse (A). She takes her normal stride to demonstrate the horse's working walk (B). She takes larger steps to demonstrate a horse's lengthened stride (C) .

Sometimes a rider thinks she is influencing the length of her horse's stride, when in reality, all she is changing is the horse's speed. To understand the difference, find a friend and try this unmounted exercise.

Lay a tape measure out in a straight line. Have your friend place her hands on her shoulders and in her "normal" walking stride, count the number of steps she takes. While she counts, watch the rate of movement of her shoulders, rather than her legs, to get a sense of her speed. Now, ask your friend to walk the same distance again, taking smaller steps (fig. 7.13 A). You will see that she maintains the same rate of movement (speed) but takes more steps to cover the same distance. Have her return to her "normal" walking stride length (fig. 7.13 B). Finally, ask her to take bigger steps; again, the number of strides used to cover the distance will decrease but her speed will stay the same (fig. 7.13 C).

You can also practice feeling the difference for yourself. Measure out a set distance and count the number of steps you take to cross it when in your "normal" stride. Then try covering the distance in shorter steps, then "normal," then longer. Feel how the rate of movement is essentially the same, even though your legs may be moving faster or slower.

THE HALF-HALT HACK

Experienced riders may recognize that some of the seat aids I am discussing in this chapter are a part of the half-halt, yet I am not addressing this more complex aid directly. Because there are many other excellent resources that break the half-halt down into quite specific detail, I will not attempt to replicate that work here.

In reality, many riders have difficulty organizing their half-halt, because its application must happen so fast. A rider may be able to effectively half-halt the horse in the walk, but in the trot or canter, she struggles to coordinate her aids with the specific fraction of the "down" beat in which the half-halt must be applied.

One of the most common challenges is that the rider holds her aids too long, thus producing a full transition rather than the more subtle rebalancing result you are usually looking for. In the world of collegiate competition, where riders must "catch-ride" anything from a high-end hunter or dressage horse to veteran "schoolies" without sophisticated training, a traditional half-halt often does not have its desired effect.

Instead, I teach riders to use the *Half-Halt Hack* (a subtle variation on the more complex half-halt aid) that can help lighten the horse's forehand or steady his tempo. The *Half-Halt Hack* is an effective way of using invisible aids to help rebalance the horse in the trot, but is less likely than a full half-halt to run the risk of creating an unintentional downward transition.

To get started, try this unmounted exercise. Stand with your feet about 3 feet apart, bend your knees and close your hips slightly, and pretend you are posting (fig. 7.14 A). As you go into the standing phase of the post, engage the IT bands on the outer part of your thigh to press your leg inward (fig. 7.14 B). Release the engagement as you enter the sitting phase. Practice going back and forth until the transition feels smooth, and notice which muscle groups in your legs are working to create the positive tension.

A

Now you are ready to try the *Half-Halt Hack* while mounted. Establish a positive, forward working trot. During the "up" beat of your post, close the upper thigh muscles as you did in the unmounted exercise above, then relax them as you sit. There should be no pinching of the knee and definitely no

7.14 A & B Emmaree prepares to practice the *Half-Halt Hack* unmounted by standing in her Athletic Stance (A). She then practices her *Half-Halt Hack* by closing her thighs as she would at the top of her post (B).

pinching of the ankle. The horse will dictate how strongly and how frequently you should repeat the squeeze, but as with any overused aid, the horse will begin to ignore the cue when the rider repeats it too much. Instead, use the *Half-Halt Hack* only at specific times—for example, during a group lesson or flat class when you are trying to hold your place on the rail.

Closing the thigh rather than going to a heavy hand to steady the tempo is more horse-friendly, looks smoother, and is more likely to get the response you want. The *Half-Halt Hack* is a handy, quick tool to help get the horse off his forehand in the trot without overdoing the aid.

when you practiced holding the abdominal contraction in the down beat of the post. If the horse is still not shortening his stride, the rider should close her fingers on the reins as if she were squeezing the water out of a sponge, while still allowing the elbow to move so the horse doesn't break to walk or even the halt. Again, when the horse finally begins to shorten his stride, the rider will feel the "punching" of his hind leg into her seat bones in the down beat of the post.

Just as in the walk, it can be hard for the rider to maintain this shortened step, so practice it only for a few strides at first. Return to working trot simply by increasing the leg pressure slightly and resuming a regular posting height.

Exercise: Shortening and Lengthening the Trot

Now that you have made some adjustments to your horse's "normal" trot in order to establish his true working trot, it is time to play with intentionally shortening and lengthening the stride. Use the same techniques just described, with your horse's active working trot as the baseline variation of the gait.

At first, riders can feel awkward or out of balance when they try to use their seat in the posting trot to influence the horse. But this is a skill that is worth the practice—many horses are quite sensitive to the rider's hand or leg aids, so having the body control to either post higher or closer to the saddle is a phenomenal tool.

7.15 A & B Olivia M. is moving her pelvis from back to front, which does not allow her to have a correct, following seat (A). Then she hovers over the saddle with a stiff back, causing her to come way out of the saddle at the canter (B).

Influencing the Canter

Finally, you are ready to try using your seat as an influencer in the canter. In this three-beat, asymmetrical gait, there is only one moment of suspension per stride. Therefore, once they have gotten past the basics, most riders find it easier to sit to the canter than to the trot. Unfortunately, whether learning to canter as a child or as an adult, many riders are taught to "polish" the saddle with their seat in the canter, rather than truly sit (fig. 7.15 A). Other riders "hover" over the saddle with a stiff back and locked joints, coming as much as 6 to 12 inches out of the saddle in each stride before slapping back down (fig. 7.15 B). Not only is this hard on the rider, it is extremely uncomfortable for the horse and can lead to resistance and other undesirable behavior, like bucking.

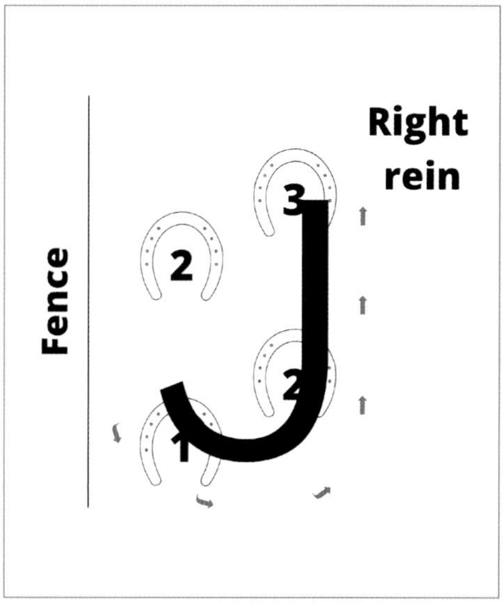

7.16 When on the right rein, think of the "following" movement of your pelvis at the canter as making the letter "J." (The arrows indicate the direction of the seat's motion.)

To fully follow the horse's back with her seat in the canter, the rider's pelvis moves in a "J" shape on the right lead, and a reversed "J" on the left. On the right lead, as the horse strikes off with the left hind, the rider's pelvis comes down, in, and forward; as the diagonal pair of legs touch down, the rider's pelvis starts moving downward to the bottom hook of the "J." As the inside fore (leading leg) reaches forward, the seat swings forward, making the stem of the "J." When the front limb strikes and pulls the horse forward, the rider's seat returns to its starting place (fig. 7.16). Of course, all of this happens much faster than any instructor can describe it!

Because the rider's seat moves so quickly through the phases of one canter stride, sometimes it is important to turn off your brain for a little bit and try to just feel the movement. Although I teach riders how their seat moves in the canter (and believe that it is important for riders to understand the mechanics), some riders can over-think this and become stiff and unyielding. A canter stride happens quickly; there is just no time for that!

If your usual way of following the canter has been to "polish" the saddle or "float" over the horse's back, when you start to use your full seat instead, you will feel muscles engaging that have previously been relaxed. In particular, you will engage the abdominal muscles at the start of the "J," then as the pelvis comes through, you will use the lower abdominals

THE ICE-CREAM-SCOOP MECHANIC

To replicate the "forward swing" feeling of an engaged seat, think of your tailbone as an ice-cream scoop. Use your abdominal muscles, without slouching over, to pull the ice-cream scoop forward (fig. 7.17 A). If you try to push the tailbone forward with your gluteal muscles, you will become stiff and tuck the tailbone too far under (fig. 7.17 B).

7.17 A Olivia M. practices her "ice-cream-scoop mechanic" by using her abdominals to pull her tailbone forward (A). Then she demonstrates the incorrect use of her ice-cream-scoop mechanic by tucking her tailbone too far under her seat (B).

and hip flexor to pull the pelvis down, in and forward as the diagonal pair touches down. As the seat comes down deeper into the saddle at the bottom of the "J," the gluteal muscles help to pull the pelvis through. When the horse brings the leading leg down, use "the ice-cream scoop mechanic" (pulling with the abdominal muscles and pushing with the gluteals) to follow the final phase of the stride (see sidebar).

Just as with the walk and trot, the canter can be ridden in the *working, lengthened,* or *shortened* variations. In general, equitation riders are not asked to demonstrate a shortened canter during a flat class or a test, but it is an important skill when it comes to jumping. Equitation riders are frequently asked to demonstrate a lengthening of the canter, as well as the hand gallop. While both of these exercises encourage the horse to take a longer stride, how the rider achieves this change is fundamentally different.

Exercise: Lengthening the Canter

During the hand gallop, the rider is in the two-point position, and actively squeezes with her legs to encourage the horse forward (fig. 7.18 A). Depending on the horse, the rider may also push her hands a few inches forward to allow for further lengthening of his back. The name "hand gallop" comes from the term "in hand," meaning a controlled gallop, as opposed to that of a racehorse, where the jockey just encourages the horse to go as fast as he can.

7.18 A & B Marin is correctly positioned in her half-seat to ask her horse for the hand gallop (A). Then she is correctly positioned in a full-seat canter and is pushing with her seat to lengthen her horse's stride (B).

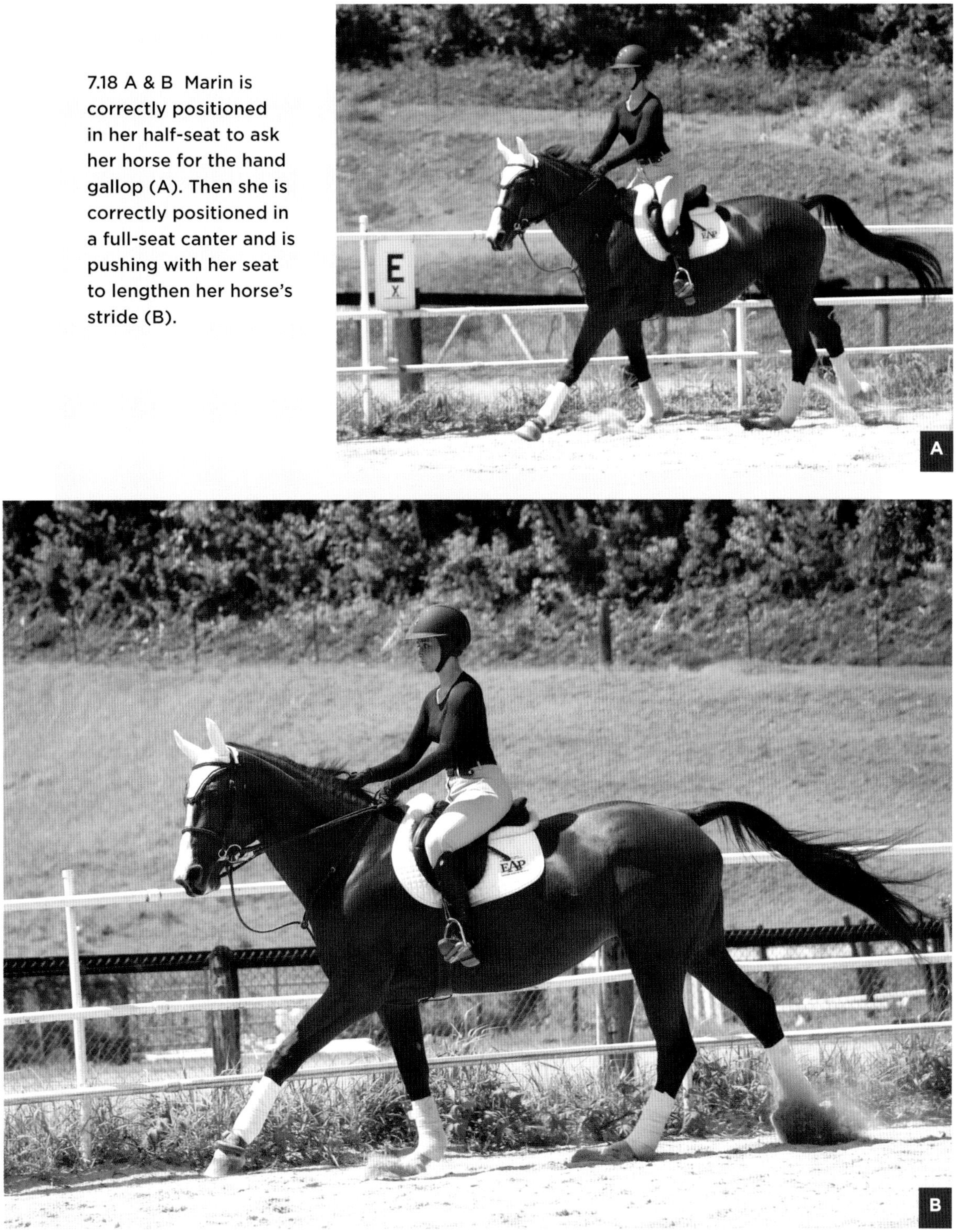

ADDITIONAL PRACTICE

One of the absolute *best* ways for a rider to really feel how her seat is moved by the horse at the walk, trot, and canter is to be longed while sitting on a vaulting surcingle (fig. 7.19 A). This specialized equipment has a large square saddle pad for the rider to sit on, and giant handles to hold onto (fig. 7.19 B). Without the impediment of the saddle, and with the horse being controlled by the person doing the longeing, most riders are able to fully engage with the feelings of movement they are experiencing.

While I personally prefer the control of having riders on the longe to a group bareback lesson, not everyone has the time, equipment, or appropriate longeing horse to try this themselves. Bareback pads usually have a handle made of heavy webbing at the withers, and if a vaulting surcingle is not available, this can be a useful alternative (fig. 7.20).

Whatever equipment you are sitting on, only practice the gaits you are comfortable with until you gain confidence and experience.

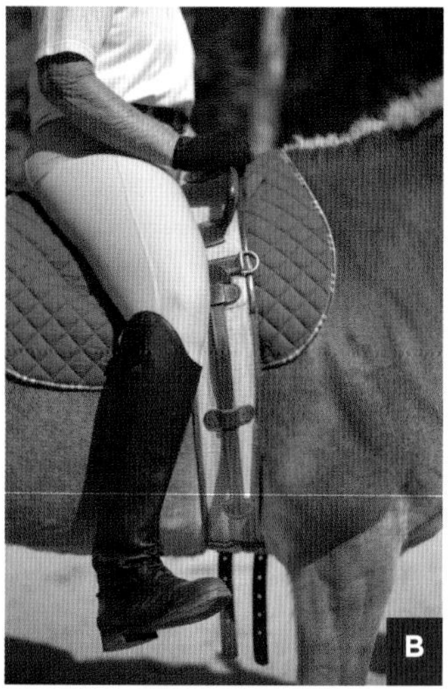

7.19 A & B Rae is being longed in a vaulting surcingle to tune into her seat's movement at the walk, trot, and canter (A). The vaulting surcingle is a great tool to teach the rider how the horse's back moves. Note the sturdy handles for the security of the rider (B).

7.20 Riding with a bareback pad is another great way for the rider to feel how the horse's back moves at the walk, trot, and canter.

By contrast, in a *lengthened* canter, the rider stays in her full seat while maintaining 5 pounds of pressure in each rein to support the horse's forehand. The rider will increase the arc of her following seat to an exaggerated "J," with a shorter movement on the hook and a longer movement on the arm (fig. 7.18 B). The ice-cream scoop mechanic will push harder in each stride, helping the horse to engage his hindquarters and pushing the stride longer from back to front. This seat movement creates an enormous amount of energy, so it is essential that the rider maintain her contact on the reins. Otherwise, the horse will lose his balance, fall to the forehand, and risk losing the lead or the gait.

Exercise: Shortening the Canter

Shortening the canter stride on the flat is how riders practice a skill they will need for jumping success. From the working canter, begin to reduce the following of the pelvis until the "J" movement becomes smaller. Take back from the elbow slightly (if the horse is quite sensitive, the rider may only need to sponge the reins) and hold the seat very still, without driving the tailbone into the saddle. The rider is still following the canter, but by constricting the abdominal muscles, she will limit how far forward the seat swings in each stride.

The most common challenge is that the rider tenses muscles that should be kept relaxed—in particular, the gluteals. Additionally, there can be a tendency to push the seat above the saddle or bring the shoulders too upright over the seat. Any of these mistakes are likely to cause the horse to break into the trot. If this happens, take a deep breath, reset, reestablish the working canter, and try again.

Once your seat is refined enough to shorten the stride in the canter, you will know that you have really done the homework required to achieve an independent, following, and elastic seat!

RIDING YOUR WAY TO BETTER DOWNWARD TRANSITIONS

Never forget! Horses are rear-wheel-drive, so they need to do both upward and downward transitions from the hind legs first. But what does this really mean? Imagine you are riding a bicycle extremely fast, then apply only the front brakes to bring it to a stop. Worst case scenario, you flip over your handlebars and, at a minimum, you are likely to get whiplash when your front tire stops suddenly while the back one keeps spinning. Horses are the same way: if you just pull with your reins, it is akin to slamming on the front brakes of your bike. Proper use of the seat helps prepare the horse to use his hind legs during the downward transition. In this section, I am going to separate several downward transitions into their essential steps.

7.21 A–C To help riders use their back more effectively, I try to pull them out of the saddle and teach them how to correctly resist (A). I place my hand right under Jinae's shoulder blades and ask her to put weight in my hand. She responds incorrectly by leaning her shoulders backward (B). Jinae has correctly dropped her weight into my hand by engaging her core (C). Now, when I try to pull her out of the saddle, I am unable to do so.

Exercise: Finding the "Drop Down" Point

Our horses do not always make it easy to ride correctly with our whole body. When a horse pulls or gets heavy in his downward transitions, many riders revert to using their arms instead of their seat. There is a spot right below the shoulder blades where the rider needs to "drop down" her weight in order to stay balanced and prevent the horse from pulling her out of the tack. To help a rider find this spot, I stand in front of the horse, hold the reins right behind the bit, and tell her to prevent me from pulling her out of the saddle (fig. 7.21 A). Usually, she resists purely in her shoulders and fists, and I am able to pull her out of the tack.

I then place my hand right below her shoulder blades and ask her to put her weight into my hand without leaning back (fig. 7.21 B). Most riders don't figure out how to do this until I tell them to use their "ice-cream-scoop mechanic" (see p. 100). Pulling the "scoop" with the lower abdominals engages the core and drops her weight down into the saddle (fig. 7.21 C). Now, when I try to pull her out of the saddle, I am not able to. Riders should use their ice-cream-scoop mechanic in every downward transition they ride.

Exercise: Walk-to-Halt Transition

Let's break down one of the most fundamental downward transitions: *working walk to halt*. The essential elements of this transition will apply to those coming out of the faster gaits as well, but in the *working walk-halt* transition, riders have more time in the movement to fully recognize what each aid is (or isn't) doing.

Start on the rail, encouraging your horse to proceed in your newly identified, active working walk. Use alternating leg pressure while maintaining a following seat and a steady 5 pounds of weight in each hand. Pick a marker ahead of you at which to execute the transition to halt. As the horse approaches the marker, focus on engaging the seat by employing the ice-cream-scoop mechanic. This will draw the pelvis forward and add depth and weight to the seat, stilling it in the saddle. Keep the shoulders stacked over the hips but maintain relaxation in the upper back. Close the fingers on the reins, applying a slight increase in pressure, and hold the elbow still. The horse should halt with his hind feet first.

If the horse doesn't halt right away, or pulls a bit on the reins, or your aids are a little mixed together at first, don't let it upset you. For many riders, applying clear, consistent aids for the transition between working walk and halt is a new challenge, and it will take some practice to get the timing, coordination, and response correct. Simply send the horse back into the working walk, review the steps in your mind, and try again.

It can be hard for a rider to feel if she is consistently using her seat as the dominant aid in this transition without having eyes on the ground. If you are practicing on your own, see if a friend can video a few transitions for you,

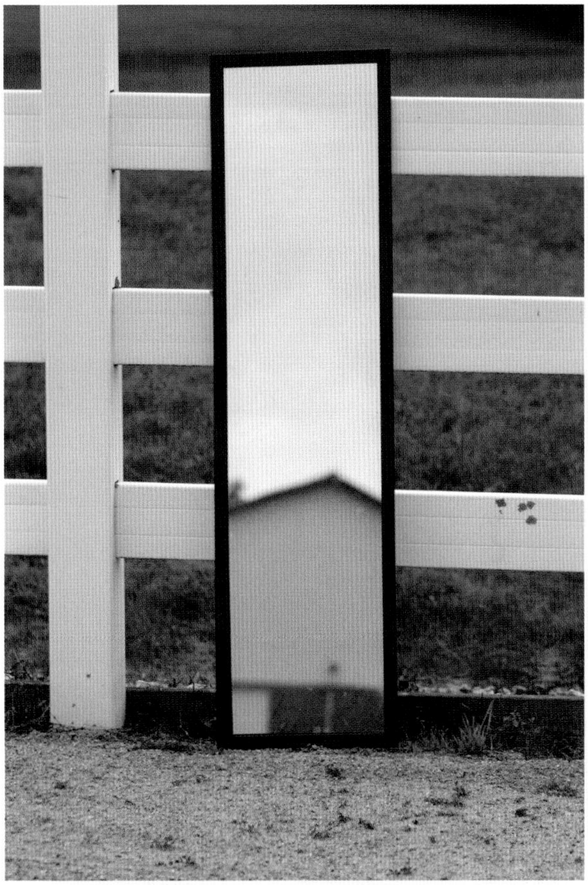

7.22 If you do not have mirrors in your indoor arena, you can buy a dressing mirror and place it on the edge of the arena to check your body alignment during transitions. Here, the mirror is placed on the ground to look at the horse's legs; it would need to be raised higher to let you see your body.

or perform the transition in front of a mirror. I have even had riders bring a portable full-length mirror to the ring (the kind most people use to check their outfits) and place it along the wall or fence so they can see what the horse's legs are doing (fig. 7.22). Remember, if the rider pulls on the reins too much, the horse's front legs will stop first.

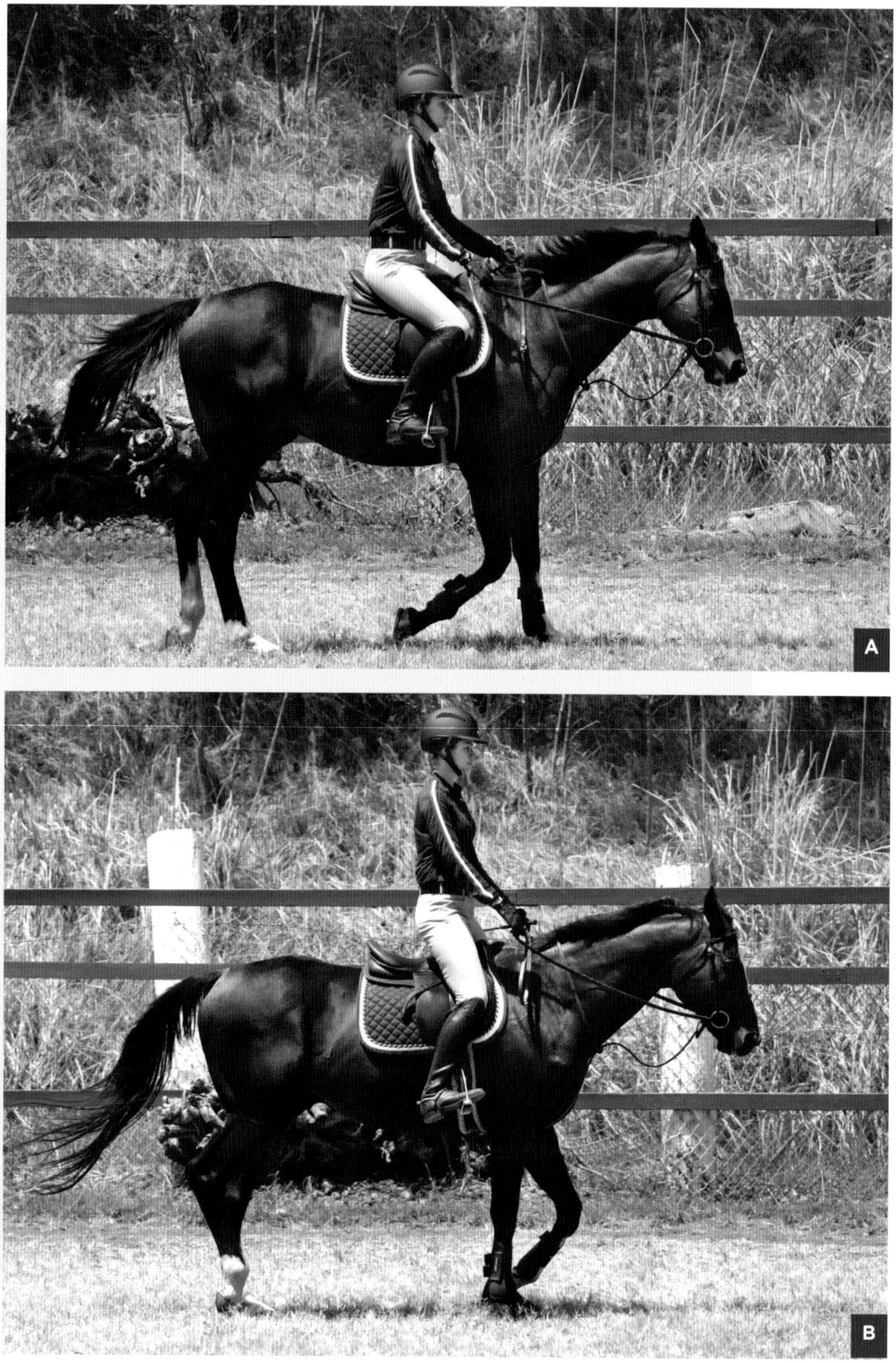

7.23 A & B
When Scarlett sits in the saddle and asks for her downward transition to the walk, her horse will be balanced and will walk from the hind end first (A). If Scarlett asks for the downward transition in the top of her post, she will not be able to use her seat to back up her hand (B).

Exercise: Trot-to-Walk Transition

Once the rider has experimented a bit with the *working walk-halt* transition, she can test her skills further by practicing the transition from *working trot* to *working walk*. The aids are essentially the same as those for the transition from *working walk* to *halt*, but the timing is quicker.

However, there is one additional (and critical) step the rider must do to move from the *posting trot* to the *working walk*—she must *sit* into the downward transition (fig. 7.23 A). When the rider skips this step, and either maintains her posting rhythm or asks for the downward transition during the "up" beat of the post, the horse may still halt. But nine times out of ten, he will do so front feet first, ending up unbalanced and on the forehand (fig. 7.23 B).

To correctly ride the transition from *working trot rising* to the *working walk*, hind feet first, perform the following steps: Sit the trot, hold the seat still, do the ice-cream-scoop mechanic, close the fingers, and still the elbow. All of this must happen within a beat or two for a prompt transition.

It is easy for the rider to tell if the horse stopped front feet first, because she will experience a moment of mini-whiplash. The rider's chest tips ahead of her pelvis, and she will need to perform a balance check.

Exercise: Canter-to-Trot Transition

In chapter 6, I broke down the *canter-to-trot* transition in some detail (see p. 78). With your increased understanding of the paces of the horse, now be sure to establish working canter as your baseline and perform transitions to working trot out of this pace. Use your ice-cream-scoop mechanic to further prepare your horse for the downward transition, and you may soon find that you hardly need to use any rein aids at all!

FINAL EXAM: SEAT CONTROL

As the rider's confidence and proficiency with these transitions grows through increased development of her seat, it is time to take a "final exam." Try to execute these downward transitions from the seat alone—no voice, and no hand. This is a great challenge to try on the longe line at first. Once you can achieve this, you will know that you have total, 100 percent control of your seat!

8

The Torture-Free Sitting Trot

"Riders, please sit the trot."

Few words can more effectively elicit an involuntary groan from a rider than these. For many riders, training their seat to follow the bounce of the horse's back in the sitting trot can seem to be an insurmountable task. But despite the challenge, there are several reasons why all riders should set a goal of improving their ability to sit the trot.

First, riders with a supple, balanced seat in the sitting trot are better able to use this tool to refine the shape, length, balance, and power of their horse's trot. Second, for riders who compete, the sitting trot is a popular test used by judges to separate a competitive equitation class, both on the flat and over fences. But perhaps most importantly, when a rider can harmoniously sit the trot, she is truly working with her horse as a partner. A supple, balanced sitting trot is a badge of honor, one that shows the rider's commitment to developing both her equitation skills and her relationship with her horse (fig. 8.1).

Developing the sitting trot is a process that takes time, and riders must be patient. The process can be challenging, and it can be frustrating, and the truth is that for some rider-athletes, the "perfect" sitting trot may never happen. But that doesn't mean a rider shouldn't work little by little to make her sitting trot the best it can be on that day, with that horse, to the best of her ability.

Some instructors struggle to describe to students exactly how to sit the trot. Instead, they offer platitudes like, "You need to relax," or "You just need to follow the horse." While both of these statements are true, it has been my experience that most students need more guidance than this to actually sit the trot effectively. Riders need to understand the mechanics of what actually happens with their bodies during a balanced sitting trot.

In chapter 7, we did this dissection for the walk, posting trot, and canter, and we are going to take that knowledge and experience with us on the journey to a torture-free sitting trot. In fact, I encourage readers to review the section of chapter 7 in which I break down the movement of the rider's pelvis in the walk (see p. 85).

To sit the trot effectively, the rider uses her gluteal muscles and the muscles of her abdominal core to stay connected with the saddle during the moment of suspension—the same muscles that control rider balance and the following movement of the pelvis in the walk. These same muscles support the torso and pelvis through the transition from the walk to the

8.1 Olivia C's supple, balanced sitting trot shows the development of both her equitation skills and her relationship with the horse.

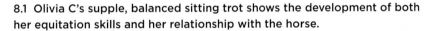

sitting trot, and help to maintain contact with the saddle throughout the trot stride.

Ready to try? Let's get started.

8.2 Jinae shows that feeling you get when you try to sit the trot and it is just not happening. Check out her horse's feelings about it!

TIP 1: FOLLOW THROUGH THE TRANSITION

When attempting sitting trot, most riders will establish the posting trot first, then transition from posting to sitting and try to find the following rhythm with their seat from there. But frequently, when a novice rider uses her leg aid to tell the horse to "go," she stiffens in other areas of her body—especially the hips and core. Now we have a situation in which the rider has squeezed or kicked her horse into the trot (and perhaps is still kicking to maintain the trot) and as she posts along, she has stiffened in every joint that needs to be supple in order to effectively sit to this bouncy gait (fig. 8.2). How well do you think the transition from posting to sitting trot will go?

8.3 Amanda closed her legs for a sitting trot while keeping her seat soft and following, leading to a harmonious sitting trot.

Exercise: Walk-to-Sitting-Trot Transition

Try this instead. Establish an active, positive, forward, working walk with a swinging, following seat, like you practiced in the last chapter (p. 87). Take a few strides with your eyes closed (if it is safe to do so) and focus on the following movement of your pelvis and seat, making the "U" shape through each stride. Now, gently cue the horse to pick up the trot, but instead of posting, focus on maintaining the following "U" shape with the seat. *Follow* through the transition and *find* your sitting trot (fig. 8.3).

It doesn't matter if the horse is not going very fast in the trot at this stage. As soon as you start to bounce, come back to the walk and try again. It doesn't matter if you only sit trot for one or two steps. What you are trying to do is retrain your brain so that the body mechanics of the walk-to-sitting-trot transition become *following* rather than *stiffening.* This process will take time.

For some riders, the idea of following through the transition with their seat is a lightbulb moment and is all the info they need to begin more effectively sitting the trot. If this is not you—keep reading.

TIP 2: DISCONNECT YOUR BRAIN

When I see a rider bouncing along in the sitting trot with a look of intense concentration on her face, I know instantly that her "thinking brain" has taken over. It is important to be familiar with the horse and rider biomechanics of the sitting trot, but only as long as this information helps the rider to understand why *following* with her seat is the most critical component to success. When a rider gets too focused on "making" her seat follow the horse, she inevitably bounces instead. When overthinking enters the picture, tension ensues, and following becomes next to impossible.

The actual movement of the seat in the sitting trot is both *side-to-side* and *forward-and-back*, which all happens far too quickly for the instructor to call out loud. The rider must experiment with the sitting trot in small doses to develop her own perception—her "feel"—for the correct movement.

SIT ON MEMORY FOAM

To determine if there is enough weight in your seat in the sitting trot, imagine that you are sitting on a piece of memory foam (fig. 8.4). As your seat follows the horse's back by making a "U" shape in each stride, picture the foam compressing beneath you just enough to leave an impression. When your weight switches to the other side, the impression will disappear.

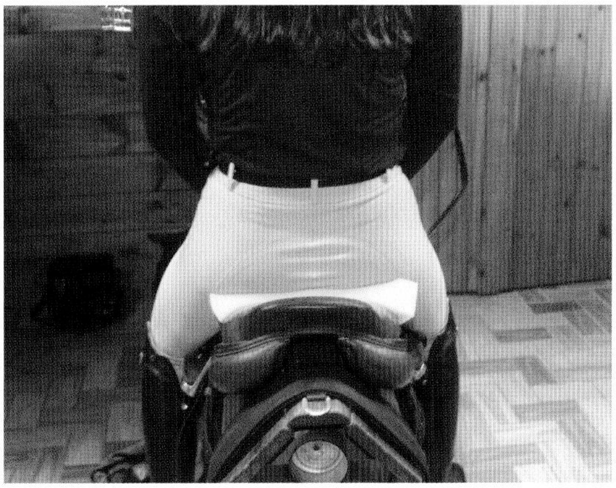

8.4 Imagine you are sitting on a piece of foam, and with each swing of your pelvis at the sitting trot, it compresses one side of the foam.

8.5 Coby goes into a hyper-relaxed arm and body position to encourage softness in her sitting trot.

Exercise: Stop Overthinking the Sitting Trot

If you are starting to overthink this movement, it is time to change things up. Return to posting trot for a few laps. Do some transitions between gaits without sitting the trot. Let your mind settle and come back to neutral before trying the sitting trot again.

Another technique that can help an overthinking rider is to let her body become like a soft rag doll. Starting in the walk (either within an enclosed arena or on the longe line), completely relax the body, releasing any muscle that is actively engaged. Allow the shoulders to slump and the arms to relax, though continue to maintain a soft, closed fist with the fingers on the reins. From this hyper-relaxed position, allow the body to follow the movement of the active working walk (fig. 8.5). Most riders will notice that their seat has become deeper and more connected to the saddle. Once the rider is comfortable with the "rag doll position" in the walk, she can try it in the sitting trot.

It can be painful for a perfectionist coach to watch, but I have found a rag doll position can produce excellent results with tense or overthinking riders. This technique is also especially helpful for an adult who has lost some of the natural elasticity of youth; in rag doll position, she can find the following movement easier than when she is sitting taller. It is as if the overall relaxation of rag doll position allows these riders to give in to the bounce of the trot, rather than resist it. Once the rider has the idea of a soft, following seat thanks to rag doll position, she should return to a correct riding posture to see if she can maintain it.

One final reminder for the overthinker: I only recommend practicing the *working walk-sitting trot* transition for between three and five minutes total per ride. These do not need to be consecutive minutes—you can weave the sitting trot practice into your other arena work for that session. What is important is to repeat the transition with a following seat over and over, with a quiet and relaxed mind, until the *following* feeling becomes your instinctive response.

TIP 3: LEARN BY WATCHING THE BEST

We all know riders we admire for their beauty and harmony on a horse. Sometimes, studying their movement during the sitting trot can help a rider better translate what her own seat should be doing. If there is an opportunity to ask an experienced rider to demonstrate both correct and incorrect sitting, novices can often better understand what is or is not working in their own attempts to sit the trot (fig. 8.6).

8.6 Sherry keeps her pelvis mobile and fluid to sit the trot.

8.7 A & B Olivia M's supple, following seat allows her to sit the trot effectively (A). Olivia M. has stiffened her spine, which causes her to bounce at the sitting trot (B).

In the sitting trot, riders must keep the pelvis mobile and fluid while the spine stays relaxed. The dynamics of sitting the trot are totally different from sitting in a chair, for example. In a chair, our spine is still from top to bottom, but there is no motion in the pelvis to challenge this stability. If we want to keep our seat stable in the sitting trot, the spine must be supported but also stay soft. Ask your experienced rider to demonstrate the difference.

After the experienced rider has warmed up her horse and herself, ask her to demonstrate a correct sitting trot. In particular, watch how her hips and lower back move through the transition into and out of the sitting position (fig. 8.7A). Next, ask her to ride with a straight spine. Immediately, you will see this experienced rider's supple, following seat begin to bounce (fig. 8.7 B). Ask her to soften her spine and you will see her melt into the saddle.

Exercise: Ride Like Your Idol

The next time you are on your own horse, take a few quiet moments to replay the movement of the experienced rider in your mind (or you can even record a video on your phone and play it back). At the halt, play with straightening your spine, feeling how doing so stiffens the joints of the torso and the muscles around them. Now, try to emulate the soft but supported spine demonstrated by the experienced rider. Take this feeling into the walk, and later into the sitting trot.

TIP 4: PRACTICE ON A CIRCLE

You might be thinking, "I couldn't possibly practice sitting trot on a circle! It is all I can do to concentrate on the following movement in my seat, and now you want me to steer, too?" But trotting on a small circle (between 10 and 15 meters in width) helps to keep the horse slow, which usually allows the rider to follow more easily than if the horse gets moving quickly down the long side (fig. 8.8).

8.8 Lexie practices her sitting trot on a 10-meter circle because the small circle aids in slowing her horse down.

8.9 In order to unlock your hips and lower back at the sitting trot, imagine you are wearing jeans. The back pockets appear and disappear from sight with each swing of the pelvis.

The circle also makes it easier to utilize this next exercise. I call it the *Back Pockets Exercise*, and it helps riders to more clearly feel the *side-to-side* and *forward-and-back* movement of their seats.

Exercise: Back Pockets

Put your horse on a 10-meter circle at the walk, and imagine that your riding pants have back pockets (fig. 8.9). Now imagine you have a friend standing in the middle of the circle. If you are correctly balanced over your seat, your friend would just be able to see the edge of your inside pocket. When the horse's inside hind goes forward, she would see the entire inside pocket and a little of the outside pocket as your hip drops down and forward. When the horse brings the inside hind back and your hip swings up and back, your friend again only sees the inside pocket's edge. This visual helps riders to unlock their hips and lower back, and encourages the correct side-to-side and forward-and-back movement of the rider's seat.

Now try this same exercise in the sitting trot. At first, you may find it difficult to get the timing right for the swing of your hips, as it all happens quite a bit more quickly in the trot than the walk. If you get out of sync, return to the walk, get centered, and try it again. With practice, you should start to feel an increased degree of control in the following motion of your seat as you "show" your pockets to the middle of the circle.

IT'S NOT ME—IT'S YOU

It is no secret that some horses' trots are easier to sit to than others—and if you have diligently worked at perfecting your sitting trot but still feel that you are not making sufficient progress, it is important to consider whether your horse's gait may be part of the problem.

There are several variables that make a horse's trot naturally smoother or bumpier. Certain breeds (Quarter Horses and many gaited breeds, for some examples) have been selectively bred for smooth, even gaits that don't tire the rider during long days in the saddle (fig. 8.10 A). These horses are somewhat easier to sit to, as the rider doesn't need to make full use of the "U" shape in her following seat.

At the other end of the spectrum are horses that travel in a fast tempo, taking shorter, quicker steps, or with a high degree of knee action (fig. 8.10 B). These qualities can be associated with certain breeds but may also be behavioral traits. Whatever the cause, the faster the horse is moving in the trot, the bumpier the gait will feel. To sit to a horse with this type of trot, the rider must fully engage her gluteal muscles, abdominals, and hip flexors—and even then, it can be difficult. This type of mover is not the ideal horse on which to learn how to sit to the trot!

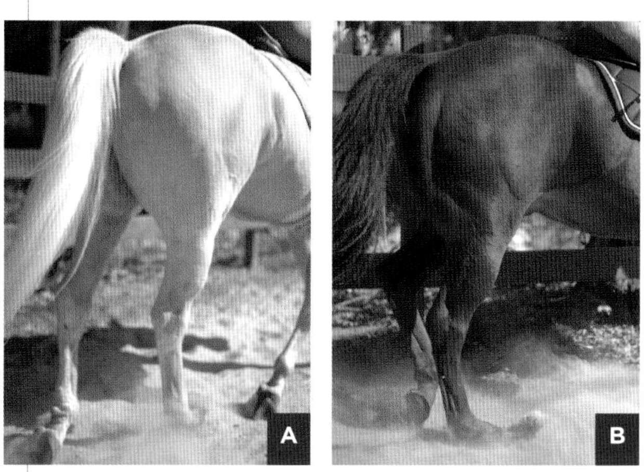

8.10 A & B It is usually easier to sit the trot on a horse with less hock and knee action because the horse's back remains on an even plane (A). A horse with higher knee and hock action requires the rider to fully engage her gluteal muscles, abdominal muscles, and hip flexors in order to sit the trot (B).

8.11 The angle of a horse's shoulder affects how bouncy his trot is. Line A represents a sloping shoulder that will be smoother, while line B represents an upright shoulder, which will be more bouncy.

Ultimately, it is the angle of the horse's shoulder that will have the most significant effect on the bumpiness of the trot. A horse with a longer, more sloping shoulder will be much smoother than a horse with a shorter, more upright shoulder. The angle of the horse's shoulder is part of his underlying conformation and, therefore, cannot be changed. When your horse has an upright shoulder conformation, it may be helpful to arrange for some practice rides on a smoother horse to help develop your following seat (fig. 8.11).

SO YOU THINK YOU CAN SIT THE TROT...

At the start of this chapter, I warned you that developing a supple, following seat in the sitting trot was a long-term project. It is the kind of skill in which progress must be measured in small steps; for example, perhaps each day or even each week you are able to sit just one more beat of trot in a row before losing the "following" mechanic. One thing is for certain: you won't get any better at it at all if you don't try.

When the day comes that you realize you are no longer feeling much concussion and you are melting into the saddle like your

COACH SALLY'S CROSSED STIRRUPS HACK

If a rider drops her stirrups, then just throws each iron over in front of the saddle, she will likely end up with big bruises on her inner thighs from the resulting "buckle bump"—not a great way of rewarding her for all that hard work!

To prevent the "buckle bump" under your thigh, try this:

1. At the halt, take your feet out of the irons.

2. Remove the extra stirrup leather from the keeper and pull the buckle down about 5 inches from the stirrup bar (fig. 8.12 A)

3. Grab the top stirrup leather and turn it upside-down so that the back of the leather is now facing up (fig. 8.12 B).

Grab the bottom stirrup leather, have it "follow" the top one, and lay both over the front of the saddle in front of the pommel (fig. 8.12 C).

Do the same with the opposite stirrup leather.

You'll find that the two sides of the stirrup leather are as flat as they can possibly be and like magic, no more bruised legs (fig. 8.12 D)!

A

experienced rider model, you are ready to try an additional challenge—the sitting trot without stirrups.

Interestingly, some riders actually find it easier to follow the trot with their seat without stirrups, as there is nothing to brace against. But for most riders, stirrups provide a sense of stability and safety, and practicing the sitting trot without them is a good check on the security of your balance and strength. Just as when you started practicing the sitting trot to begin with, take it in small doses, focusing on following the transition from working walk to sitting trot with your supple seat. For your horse's sake,

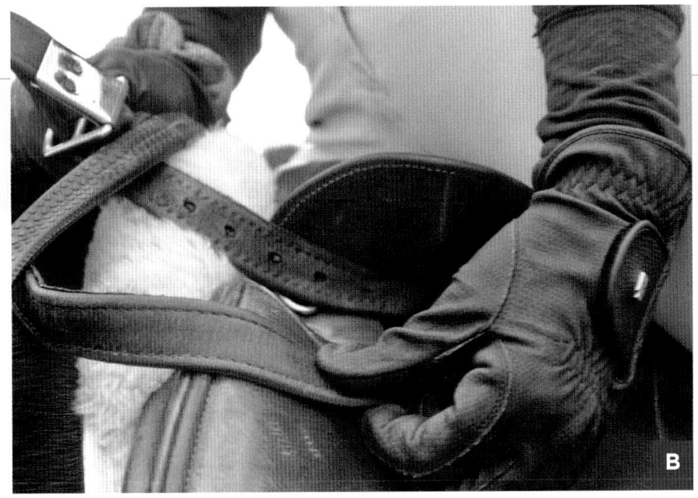

8.12 A–D When you are ready to try the sitting trot without stirrups, try my Crossed Stirrups Hack to avoid bruised inner thighs. First, remove your foot from the stirrup and pull down the buckle (A). Next, turn over the top leather so the underside of the leather is facing up (B). This step is key to smooth crossed stirrups. Once the top leather is turned upside down and laid flat, follow it with the bottom leather and lay it flat (C). When your stirrups are crossed correctly with my Crossed Stirrups Hack, the saddle skirt will lie flat and no more bruised inner thighs (D)!

SITTING TROT ON THE EQUITATION CATCH RIDE

For hunter seat equitation riders and those interested in scholastic or collegiate catch ride competition, the sitting trot is a "must have" skill at every level beyond introductory. In equitation, the rider's position should work effortlessly and the aids must be invisible; showing a large following motion in the sitting trot is not desired. Successful equitation riders have learned how to sit the trot so they appear totally still. However, these riders are not fully into their seat at all, and instead are using a variation I call the "light-seat sitting trot."

At first, a light-seat sitting trot may seem to be the opposite of what I have described in this chapter, but think of it instead as a technique to use under specific circumstances. When catch riding at scholastic or collegiate shows, the rider really doesn't know what kind of horse she will get. Many horses used at these competitions are veteran lesson horses that were never fancy enough to compete or retired show horses that don't move as smoothly as they once did. Riders often find themselves trying to demonstrate sitting trot on a horse that feels like a jackhammer, which isn't fun for the rider or the horse.

In my program, I start by teaching riders at all levels how to develop a deep, following sitting trot. This teaches riders a fundamental understanding of the biomechanics

8.13 Gabby demonstrates a light-seat sitting trot.

required in sitting trot, and produces the strength, control, and sense of the horse's movement necessary for success. Only once these fundamentals are in place is a rider ready to learn how to perform the *light-seat sitting trot* for the equitation ring, in which she "contains the follow."

In the light-seat sitting trot, the rider quiets her hips by slightly engaging her abdominal core and upper inner thigh muscles. She is still following the "U" of the trot rhythm, but she is doing so in a more subtle way. This technique is quite similar to the one you practiced earlier to change the length of your horse's stride in the walk, now applied to the sitting trot. Usually, riders need to roll slightly more forward on the pelvis to get the right effect, which will lighten the seat. Be sure to keep the hips square (fig. 8.13).

The light-seat sitting trot will require some practice to get the balance of aids correct. The most common mistake is that the rider holds her hips too still, causing the horse to break to walk—a major equitation-ring fault. It can be helpful at this stage to have an experienced friend watch from the ground to offer feedback, or to ask a friend to take a short video. Ideally, the trot remains the same speed whether the rider is sitting or posting, and the rider absorbs the trot energy through her elastic hips and soft spine—in a more subtle, less busy, manner.

practice sitting trot without stirrups for no more than five minutes per session. Always cross the stirrups in front of the saddle.

If you have the opportunity, having someone longe you on a quiet, steady horse allows you to concentrate just on your seat. I have also had good success longeing riders using a vaulting surcingle, as its large, sturdy handles provide the rider with good support, which increases her confidence.

Despite the fact that developing a correct sitting trot can be tedious, the ultimate goal of having a "good seat" cannot happen without skill in the sitting trot. When a judge says that a rider has a good seat, she doesn't mean that the rider is just hanging on well. A rider with a good seat is moving with the horse, and her seat is kind to the horse. She is working in harmony with the horse's rhythm, instead of being out of sync and bouncing above him. Having a good seat will improve every aspect of rider/horse communication.

COACH SALLY'S TOP 10 TIPS

Tip 8: Be a Leader, Not a Follower

Back when I was recruiting student athletes to the Dartmouth equestrian team, I often was asked to make decisions based on a student's riding video and resume alone. While these tools told me about her equestrian skills, I was also interested in learning about her activities and volunteerism outside of the saddle. In particular, I looked for signs of growth; for example, as a freshman, she was a member of an organization, but by the time she became an upperclassman, she was a leader.

What did this information tell me about her chances of being successful on the equestrian team? More than anything, it showed me her inner drive.

My favorite riders of all time possessed three essential qualities: a desire to learn, a desire to improve, and a desire to continuously progress. When these riders were done with their team practice and had five minutes to spare before heading back to campus, they could be found ringside watching the next lesson. These riders bought into what I was teaching them and applied every lesson to their practice, every ride.

This is the kind of rider I would like you to be—one with an insatiable desire to grow and learn, one who will transition over time from an "interested follower" to a true leader in the sport.

8.14 My ideal riders possess three essential qualities: a desire to learn, a desire to improve, and a desire to continuously progress. Many of my Dartmouth Equestrian Team riders possessed these qualities, which allowed them to be true leaders in the sport.

9

The Biomechanics of Bending

Now that you have better awareness of your basic aids, it is time to focus on how to use those aids to correctly ride one of the most common arena figures—the circle. For the athletic equestrian, there is a difference between simply steering the horse onto a circle shape and actually *riding* a circle. The most effective riders use their own biomechanics, supported by their natural aids, to help bend a horse's body in the direction of movement. Think of creating a truly round circle as the final exam to assess if the rider's aids are coordinated and effective (fig. 9.1).

9.1 Lauren's horse is bent correctly to the inside on a circle on the right rein.

Why does riding a correctly bent circle matter so much? Left to his own choice, the horse will lean onto his inside shoulder and counter-bend his body to the outside of the circle (fig. 9.2). But because the rider's weight makes the horse top-heavy, a horse

9.2 Lauren's horse is bent incorrectly to the outside on a circle on the right rein.

that does not bend properly on circles and turns can overload his forehand, predisposing him to lameness over time. In everything you do with your horse—transitions, lateral work, even hacking out—the horse must be balanced and true beneath the rider in order to achieve ultimate harmony.

Further, in the hunter seat world, or for balanced seat riders interested in eventing, what we are ultimately working toward is the ability to jump a course. In asking a horse to correctly bend his body on a circle, we are laying the foundation to smoothly ride through the corner from one line of jumps to the next (fig. 9.3). The hind legs of the horse must track in a straight line behind the forelegs, with an equal degree of push power coming from each side of the horse's body.

Bending a horse correctly requires the rider to consistently and effectively maintain the outside supporting aids, both on the flat and over fences. Developing this skill will rapidly increase the rider's ability to maintain precise control of her horse's line.

Accomplishing a truly straight track with the horse is not easy to achieve, for several reasons. Just like humans, horses are naturally asymmetrical and have a dominant side. It is only through progressive training that they develop more equal suppleness, strength, and coordination on both sides of the body. Additionally, a rider who does not sit straight on the horse will cause inconsistencies in the horse's movement; sometimes a horse moves on a straight track with one rider but becomes crooked with another.

Earlier in this book, I discussed using a raked stretch of the arena to determine whether the horse's hind feet were stepping behind, into, or in front of the print left by the front foot on the same side (p. 87). If you used this technique, you may have noticed that the prints of the hind feet came to the inside or outside of those left by the front legs (fig. 9.4). Or perhaps you noticed that when tracking right, your horse moved in a working walk, but when you tracked left, he moved with a shortened or lengthened stride. These are examples of asymmetry in the horse, and although each of these issues requires a different fix, this information will prove useful as we begin to incorporate lateral work into the horse's training program.

Lateral movements are a series of progressive exercises through which a rider encourages the horse to use his body from side to side as well as from back to front. When I ask riders to name the simplest lateral movement, most will answer "leg-yield," which is a reasonable guess as we teach basic leg-yielding to the horse fairly early in his career. But in practice, the circle is the most basic lateral movement, and a rider must have this figure well in hand before moving on to more complex lateral exercises.

9.3 Marin's horse is balanced and bending correctly to the inside as she goes from one line of jumps through the corner to the next. The hind legs must track in a line behind the forelegs with an equal degree of pushing power coming from each side of the horse's body.

9.4 When viewing your raked arena, you can check if your horse is traveling straight. Here, the hind hoofprints fall to the inside and slightly behind the front hoofprints, which shows us that the horse is not traveling straight.

BENDING BASICS

Before performing any lateral work, it is important that the horse has a proper warm-up. Stretching cold muscles, whether they belong to horse or human, is an easy way to cause injury. Younger, athletic, or fitter horses may

THE FIVE REIN AIDS

The rider's hand can be one of her most useful natural aids. Riders who have developed a steady base of support and are progressing toward independence in their aids are ready to begin to use their hands in a much more nuanced and refined way than the beginner. This includes understanding the functional differences among the five principal rein aids: the *direct rein*, the *indirect rein,* the *supporting (bearing) rein*, the *leading (opening) rein,* and the *pulley (emergency) rein*.

The *direct rein* is the most basic rein aid, and it is used for steering and control. A direct rein is any pressure or tension on the rein that is coming straight back from the bit to the rider's hand to her elbow (fig. 9.5 A).

An *indirect rein* is when the rider takes the rein pressure from one side of the horse to the other, such as when the rider's right hand brings the rein pressure across toward her left hip (or vice versa). The indirect rein can be used by experienced riders to shift the weight and balance of the horse onto the opposite side of his body in lateral work (fig. 9.5 B). When the pressure is brought across in front of the withers, the horse's weight will shift to his opposite front leg; when the pressure is brought behind the withers, the horse's weight shifts to his opposite hind leg.

However, it is easy for a rider to accidentally misuse the indirect rein, and cause the horse's weight to shift unintentionally. I hardly ever teach riders to use the indirect rein and see it most often used (incorrectly). *Wrist Magic Bands* (p. 59) are a useful tool to alert a rider if she is unintentionally crossing her hand to the opposite side of the horse.

By contrast, the *supporting (bearing rein)* is one of my favorite rein aids, and it plays a critical role in helping to control the outside of the horse's body when turning or circling. English riders, who use their rein aids independently, often use the supporting rein in combination with another rein aid. For example, the rider uses an inside direct rein to indicate direction, and uses an outside supporting rein to prevent the horse's shoulder from swinging by placing her rein against the horse's neck without letting her hand cross over (fig. 9.5 C).

Western riders, who hold both reins in one hand and use them together, would call this a *neck rein*.

9.5 A–D The direct rein is the most basic rein aid and is used for steering and control (A). The indirect rein is pressure from one rein to the opposite front or hind leg (B). I rarely teach this to riders because it is easy to misuse and miscue the horse. The supporting (bearing) rein plays a critical role in helping to control the outside of the horse's body (C). The opening (leading) rein essentially leads the horse's nose in the direction the rider wants him to go (D). Jinae demonstrates the pulley (emergency) rein by planting her left hand on the horse's neck and pulling up and back with the right rein (E). The pulley rein can aid the rider in slowing down or stopping a horse.

The *leading (opening) rein* is most useful for young or green horses who do not yet understand a direct rein. The rider "opens" her hand by bringing it anywhere from 6 to 12 inches away from the horse's neck, essentially "leading" his nose in the direction she wants him to go (fig. 9.5 D).

The leading rein can also be a useful tool when schooling at home, even with an experienced horse, if he has gotten "stuck" and won't go forward. For example, perhaps the horse is reluctant to go through a puddle in the ring. Instead of just kicking the horse, the rider can use her leg and a leading rein together to help the horse get moving without accidentally pulling back or otherwise restricting him.

When using the leading rein, the rider must be careful to keep her thumbs up and angled slightly toward each other; do not allow the wrist to flip or rotate. The leading rein is not an ideal technique for the equitation ring, where aids are meant to be invisible, unless the rider is encountering significant resistance in the horse and there are no other alternatives.

The *pulley (emergency) rein* is an important tool for a rider to learn somewhat early in her career, though it is not appropriate for a total beginner. I want riders to be fairly comfortable with this technique before they begin jumping or riding extensively out in the open, as it can be an effective method of slowing or even stopping a horse who has become overly exuberant.

A pulley rein can also function as an extra half-halt if a horse becomes too heavy on the forehand on course, and there is no time to ride a transition. To use the pulley rein in this situation, the rider will plant her outside hand on the horse's neck, anchor her seat in the saddle, and use a quick up-and-back pressure on the inside rein.

In contrast, the hand position is reversed if the horse has become too fast or the rider is losing control; the goal is to bring the horse to the halt. The inside hand is planted on the horse's neck, and it is the outside hand that quickly pulls up and back while the rider anchors her seat in the saddle (fig. 9.5 E). This action will elevate the horse's head and neck and turn him away from the direction of movement; if you are riding in an arena, the pulley rein will turn the horse toward the perimeter fence or wall. These shifts in the balance and direction of the horse's movement usually enable the rider to ultimately bring him back to a halt.

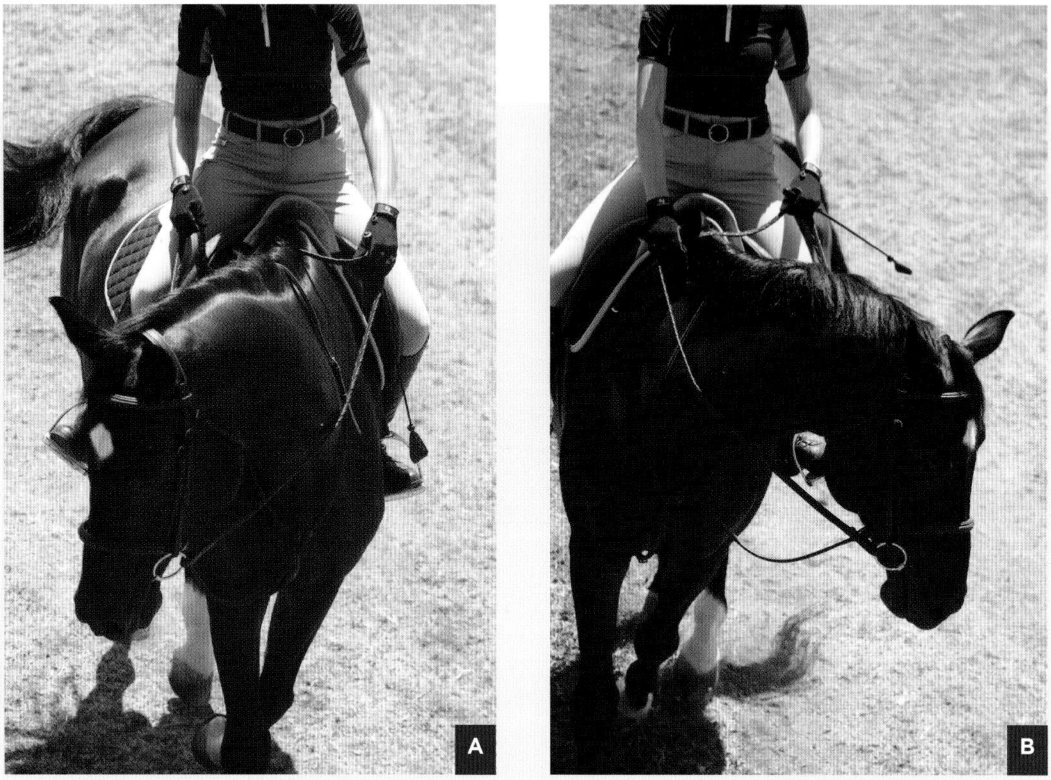

9.6 A & B "Springing" is a dynamic stretch for the horse's neck and body. Here the horse is springing to the right (A) and the left (B). You should start your springing exercise at the walk and also do it at the trot once the horse is used to the aids.

be capable of lateral work sooner in their ride than older, stiffer, or unfit horses. Once the horse's basic warm-up is complete, one helpful exercise to prepare him for lateral work is called "springing." Springing is a dynamic stretch for the horse's neck in which the rider will gently take him through the range of motion required for the day's work.

Exercise: Springing

To introduce the horse to *springing*, begin at the working walk and ride down the long side of the arena, tracking left. Take your right elbow back, using a *direct* rein, applying just enough pressure that you can see the horse's right eye. Hold the horse's neck in this counter-flexed position for half of the long side, then gently release (fig. 9.6 A). Ride through the short end, then take your left elbow back, until you can see the horse's left eye (fig. 9.6 B). Hold for half the arena, then gently straighten.

When you ask for inside flexion, at first your horse may think you want him to turn and cut across the arena. To prevent this mistake, gently close the inner thigh and calf muscles, making your leg a barrier that the horse can't press through. If the horse is quite green, stick with just counter-flexion until he has more experience.

Repeat the springing exercise on both reins, gradually increasing the length of time you hold the stretch until the horse can maintain it for the entire long side. Once horse and rider are both comfortable with springing, they can practice it in the rising trot as well. Overall, this process should take no more than five minutes.

When springing, the horse will almost certainly find one direction easier to turn his neck in than the other. In this way, springing can help riders to identify their horse's stiff side versus his soft side. However, if the horse is naturally quite supple, he may find springing in either direction fairly easy.

To determine which side is which for a more ambidextrous horse, come to the halt and gently ask him to turn his neck toward your knee. See how far the horse can turn his neck before he must step out with the outside hind to catch his balance, and compare this stretch to the opposite side. If your horse can touch your right knee without stepping out behind when you turn his neck right, but can only get halfway to your knee when you turn his neck left, then his left side is the "soft" side and his right side is the "stiff" or "hard" side (fig. 9.7).

Exercise: Map Out a Circle

Once the horse is warmed up and loose, it is time to check in with the bending aids. To get started, map out a 20-meter circle in your arena. The easiest way to do this is to use a cone that marks the circle's center, then place four more cones evenly around the circle, each 10 meters from this central point. If you ride in an arena with dressage letters, these can also be used to determine a 20-meter diameter, so long as they have been properly measured out. When I am teaching and don't have cones available, I will

9.7 I am helping Olivia M. figure out which side her horse's soft side is and which is his hard side. Working your horse's muscles equally will help all of his gaits be more regular and even.

9.8 A & B In order to help the rider visualize a 20-meter circle, I pace out 10 meters and stand there as a visual point for the rider to make the 20-meter circle around me (A). I stand in the center of a 20-meter circle so that Olivia M. has a reference for the size of her circle (B).

walk the distance of 10 meters on foot from the wall or fence, and will stand at that point (fig. 9.8 A). The rider then has at least one point of visual reference for the radius of her circle (fig. 9.8 B).

Now you are ready to create a correct circle on horseback!

Exercise: Ride the Bend

At a working walk, begin riding the 20-meter circle you have mapped out. Ask the horse to bend as follows: Use an inside direct rein to guide the horse onto the circle and to encourage him to look to the inside, while maintaining an outside supporting rein so that he cannot pop his neck and shoulder out of the circle. Apply a steady, gentle pressure with your inside leg at the girth, giving the horse a point to bend his body around (fig. 9.9 A), and draw the outside leg slightly behind the girth to prevent the horse's hindquarters from swinging out (fig. 9.9 B).

The position of the rider's outside leg is actually quite similar to the canter cue, but while the canter cue is a highly active leg aid, in bending, the outside supporting leg is a more consistent pressure of the entire calf, from top to bottom. If your horse overreacts to the outside supporting leg and is trying to transition to canter, try just closing your outside thigh against the saddle and see if that does the trick (fig. 9.10). Your eyes should remain softly looking around the circle, not down or overly positioned to the inside.

9.9 A & B Lexie's inside leg is on the girth, acting as a pole for the horse's rib cage to bend around (A). Lexie's right leg is slightly back to keep the horse's haunches from swinging out on her turn to the left (B).

The bend required of the horse on a 20-meter circle is minimal, and even stiff horses are usually able to offer a somewhat correct response to the rider's bending aids. Therefore, remember that the bend of the horse's body will be correct when the rider's aids are correct. When the rider tries to create bend by just pulling on the inside rein, the horse's hind end will swing outward, leaving the track of the front legs until the horse's body is moving on three or four separate tracks.

9.10 Alexa has closed both her outside thigh and calf to prevent her horse's haunches from swinging to the right on her left-hand turn.

If you are working on your own, it can be difficult to feel the position of the horse's hind legs on a 20-meter circle at the walk.

9.11 To test what it feels like to go into a circle with incomplete aids, Coby slumps over into her rag doll position and will pull with the inside rein only, with no leg aids. Most likely her horse will fall onto his inside shoulder.

Therefore, we are now going to intentionally apply our aids *incorrectly* in order to develop a sense of what losing the horse's hindquarters to the outside feels like.

Decrease the size of the horse's circle until it is 10 meters wide. A smaller circle requires a greater degree of bending from the horse, so chances are that he will bring the hindquarters to the outside in order to avoid the work of bending. But the rider is going to *ensure* that this happens by going into a rag doll position (see p. 112) with her body and pulling on the inside rein (fig. 9.11). Almost immediately, she should feel as if the horse's hind end has disappeared out from beneath her.

For riders who have not practiced feeling the horse's hind end before, the effect of its loss is revelatory. Once the horse loses his

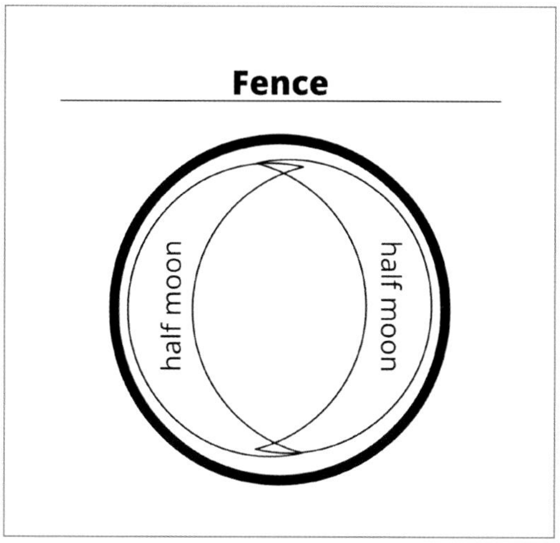

9.12 To make a round circle, I imagine the complete circle is made up of two half moons.

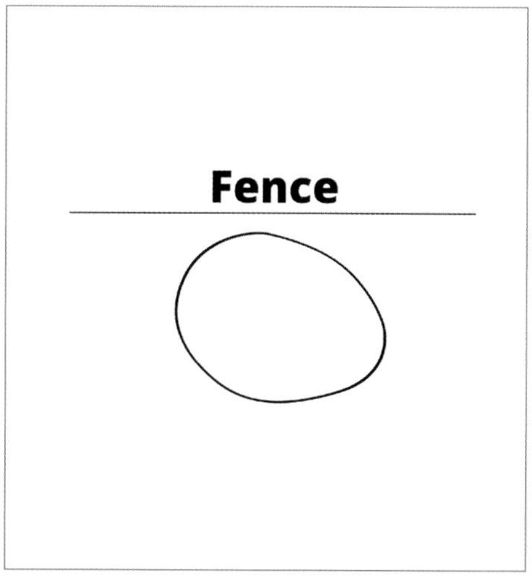

9.13 A common fault of the circle shape is a correct half moon to start, while the second half collapses.

hindquarters to the outside of the circle, it takes twice as much work to get them back on track. When the rider knows what it feels like to lose the horse's hindquarters, she is better able to actively ride to prevent the hind end from sliding to the outside in the first place.

Exercise: More Advanced Bending

Now that you have a general idea of how the bending aids work (and what can happen if the rider fails to provide enough support on the outside of the bend), it is time to take it to the trot. Return to the 20-meter circle, making sure that the horse remains consistently 10 meters away from the center point. It can help to think of the circle as two half-moons joined together; concentrate on riding each half-moon accurately and it will result in a round, even circle (fig. 9.12). A common mistake is that the first half-moon is round while the second one becomes flat (fig. 9.13). This means that the rider stopped using her active inside leg aid on the second half of the circle.

Continue to practice riding circles all over the arena, focusing both on accuracy in the shape and application of the aids. As you begin to ride 20-meter circles without the benefit of the marker cones, still try to imagine those four points in your mind's eye. As you navigate the circle, your eyes should always be focused on the next point. If you struggle with this (and many riders do), *Eyes-Up Goggles* (p. 70) can be a helpful tool.

As you get more experienced using your bending aids to shape and support the horse

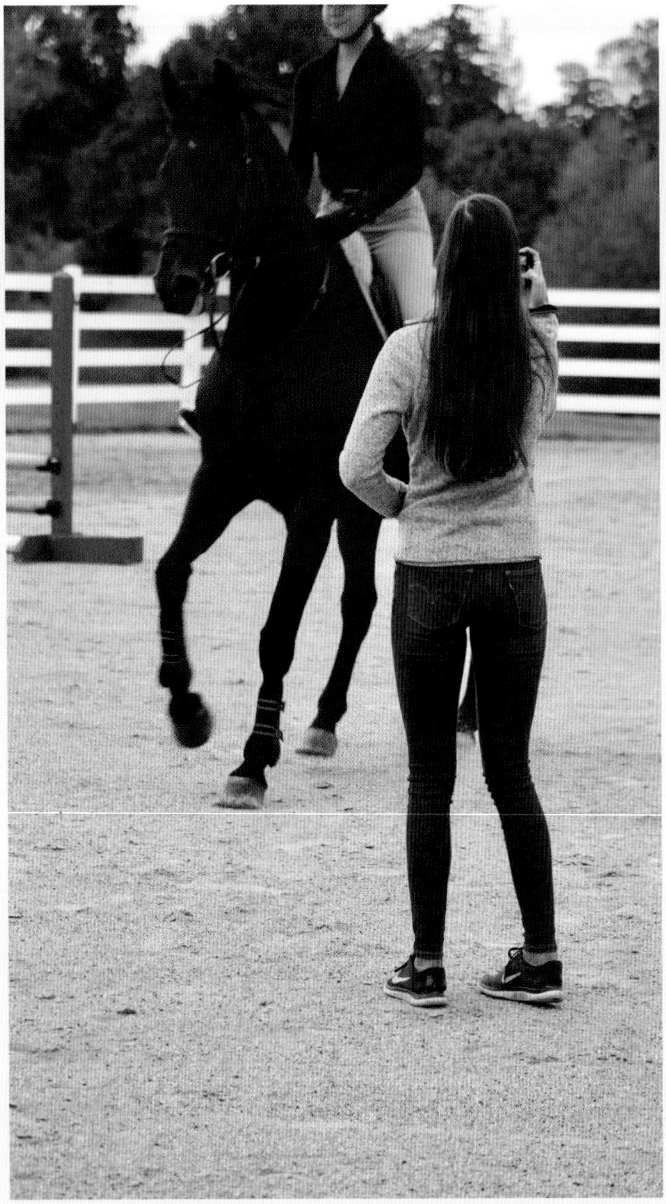

9.14 Teagan takes video of Olivia M's outside aids so she can make sure she is using them correctly.

on the 20-meter circle, challenge yourself to achieve the same response on a smaller circle—15 meters is a good size to start with. When riding trot circles smaller than 20 meters, try using the sitting trot. When you post, every beat in which the seat is lifted is a lost opportunity to feel the horse beneath you, so remaining in the sitting trot gives you more information about the horse's alignment than posting. Have a friend stand on the outside of the circle (or take a video) to make sure that your outside aids remain active and supportive on the smaller circle (fig. 9.14).

Exercise: Figure Eights

Another fun challenge is to try turning the individual circles into a figure eight. Figure eights are not only a superb test for rider accuracy in maintaining the horse's track, but a coordination challenge as the inside/outside aiding switches from one side of the rider's body to the other within just a few strides. Figure eights should look like two even, round circles joined at the centerline (fig. 9.15 A), not a pair of tear drops (fig. 9.15 B).

To help with accuracy, we are going to borrow a concept from our dressage-loving friends—the letter "X." Dressage riders use the imaginary letter "X" to mark the dead center of the riding arena, and they use this point to help place various figures and movements. For our purposes, "X" can be a fixed point anywhere along the center line of the

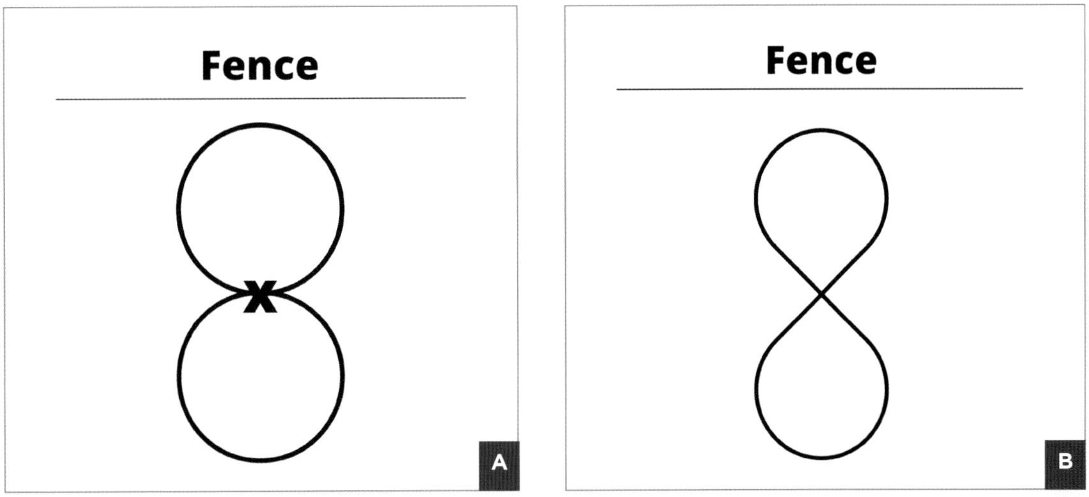

9.15 A & B A correct figure eight consists of two circles joined at the center (A). An incorrect figure-eight looks like two teardrops joined across the diagonal (B).

arena, but this point will mark the center of the figure eight.

At first, it can be helpful to choose an imaginary point that is in alignment with two other fixed points that are directly opposite each other along the edge of the arena (such as fence posts, beams, or dressage letters), or place a cone or other small object to help mark "X" itself. After a little bit of practice, most riders find that they are able to visualize their center "X" without as many external tools. I will use "X" in the rest of my instructions here to indicate the center point of your figure eight.

Your first figure-eights will be two 20-meter circles connected at "X," oriented along the length of the arena. Begin tracking left, turn off the rail, and start a 20-meter circle at "X." Maintain clear inside positioning in the horse and allow your eye to softly lead you around the circle.

As you approach "X" to finish the left circle, shift your eye to the second point of the right-hand circle (the first point is, of course, "X," which is also the last point of your first circle).

Ride at least one straight stride over "X," sit a beat to change the posting diagonal, and switch the roles of your inside and outside leg and rein aids. Now, your right leg is initiating the inside bend in the horse's body, your right direct rein is indicating direction, and your left rein and leg together provide support on the horse's outside. Continue around the circle tracking right, eyes leading the way.

As you return to "X," now shift your eye to the second point of the left-hand circle, ride at least one straight stride, sit a beat to change the

9.16 Gaby at the start of her first circle of her figure eight. As she leaves the rail to start the figure, she is looking to the left and bending her horse around her inside leg in order to start her first circle.

posting diagonal, and switch the roles of your inside and outside leg and rein aids yet again. Ideally, there is no change of rhythm or energy in the gait, and the horse smoothly switches from one bend to the other (fig. 9.16).

Once the 20-meter figure eight feels easy and fluid, you and your horse are ready for the ultimate bending challenge: a figure eight with 10-meter circles. This is one of the most common individual equitation tests, and it is amazing how many riders perform this figure incorrectly. The 10-meter figure eight will be oriented along the short side of the arena, and you will use the centerline to help define the starting and ending points.

It can be helpful to try the figure in the walk first before moving to the sitting trot. Start by riding positively forward down the centerline of the arena. When you get to your starting point, begin a smooth, even 10-meter circle to the left. Keep your eyes leading you around the figure, with steady supporting outside aids.

As you approach "X," you will straighten the horse for one stride, shift your eyes right, and change the orientation of the inside and outside aids. Continue looking around with your eyes to the right until you approach "X," then shift your eyes left and change the orientation of inside and outside aids again to begin another figure eight. Alternatively, plan and execute a transition to the halt at "X" as you complete the second circle, centering your body directly over the point at which the two circles connect.

COACH SALLY'S TOP 10 TIPS

Tip 9: Pay Attention to Detail

For me, practicing attention to detail is a skill that must be cultivated from a rider's very first lessons until it becomes a habit that she applies to all aspects of her horsemanship. It shows everyone watching that a rider is serious and committed to her sport (fig. 9.17).

Before she mounts, a rider should check to ensure that the girth is snug, all leather straps on the bridle are tucked into their keepers and runners, and that the saddle pad is pulled up into the gullet. Ensure the reins and stirrup leathers are free from twists. After mounting, stirrup adjustments should be made with the foot still in the stirrup, and the excess leather run though the keeper on the saddle and tucked under the flap. No piece of equipment should be left loose to bounce around, where it will annoy the horse and distract the eye.

Whether schooling or competing, riders should select traditional attire that is well-fitting. Boots should be polished, clothing should be clean, and shirts tucked in. Gloves should fit well and be dark in color. Belts should be worn with the buckle rotated to the side of the hip so that it does not protrude from the jacket. Helmet chin straps should *always* be in contact with the rider's chin. When competing, before you enter the ring, have your coach or a friend wipe the dust from your boots, and check to ensure that your coat lapels are flat, your helmet is level, and your number centered on your back (fig. 9.18).

9.17 Attention to detail is a skill that must be cultivated from a rider's very first lesson. Eliza has her hair braided, her shirt tucked in and well-fitting breeches, boots, and gloves, and is ready for her lesson.

9.18 Nathalie is perfectly turned out for a collegiate competition.

Once you are in the saddle, review your coach's instructions and follow through on them to the best of your ability. Don't make excuses; instead, try your hardest each day, each ride, to practice what you are taught. Details matter.

9.19 Olivia M. has dropped her eyes down, which could cause her upper body to tip forward.

TROUBLESHOOTING THE BEND

Several common rider faults can interfere with the horse's ability to properly bend. One of the most common is the rider who overlooks with her eyes on the circle. Instead of allowing her eyes to softly lead her horse to the next point, she turns her entire head to the inside, sometimes so much that her chin is over her shoulder (fig. 9.19). This causes the rest of her alignment to shift, tipping her weight to the horse's inside shoulder and usually causing her to stop supporting with the outside aids. The horse's haunches swing to the outside of his track, losing the alignment in his body that she is seeking to maintain.

A less extreme eye-related fault is the rider who drops her eyes down, looking over the horse's inside shoulder and into the dirt. Earlier,

9.20 Olivia M. is demonstrating the "hand-dropper" by overusing the inside rein, which causes her to lock the inside elbow.

you learned that when the rider looks down it often leads to her head tipping forward and her upper body coming ahead of the ideal vertical alignment (see p. 68). To compensate, her body pinches at the knee, rendering both the driving and supporting leg aids ineffective. The horse's impulsion decreases and the rider's ability to coordinate independent aids is lost. Again, regular practice with *Eyes-Up Goggles* can help correct each of these eye-related bad habits.

One of the most common rein faults is what I call the "hand-dropper" (fig. 9.20). This rider is properly supporting with her outside aids, but either overuses the inside rein, pulling the horse's neck too much to the inside, or drops her hand down and straightens and locks the inside elbow. In both situations, the rider is pulling back without elasticity on the inside rein while restricting with the outside aids, giving the horse no real choice except to resist. This rider will benefit from riding with *Elbow Magic Bands* to regain the soft, following, elastic position in her arms.

Riding a circle with correct bending is one of the first major challenges to a novice rider learning to independently coordinate her aids. Perhaps it should come as no surprise, then, that another common challenge is the rider who overthinks, or who is concentrating so hard on her bending aids that she neglects to maintain correct, centered posture.

Sometimes a rider takes this to an extreme,

collapsing in her core, hunching forward with the upper body and taking the lower leg off. Teaching Tools such as *Flat-Back Roll-Ups* (p. 67) and *Elbow Magic Bands* (p. 54) can provide a tactile reminder for these riders to maintain positive muscle engagement in their trunk while also working toward independence with their natural aids (fig. 9.21).

One final common challenge is the horse that breaks gait when asked to bend on the circle. While at first this might seem to be a horse-related problem, it is more often the result of a rider who has allowed the circle to become too small (and is, therefore, increasing the degree of bend required of the horse), or a rider who has failed to maintain an active, driving leg aid. We often use a well-placed circle to help slow a horse that has become too quick; therefore, if the rider fails to indicate to the horse that he should maintain the gait he is currently working in while also creating bend on the circle, breaking is a common response. Riders must maintain accuracy and active aids to prevent the break.

9.21 Olivia M. rides with her *Eyes-Up Goggles* and *Flat-Back Roll-Ups* to help correct her aids on the circle.

FINGERS-CLOSED BALLS

In order to use any rein aid correctly, the rider's hands must be kept closed around the reins, the fingertips on each hand touching the palm. But many riders struggle to maintain this consistent, soft fist around the rein, no matter how many times their instructor reminds them. My solution? *Fingers-Closed Balls.*

A *Fingers-Closed Ball* is a soft, foam ball around 1 to 2 inches in diameter that the rider carries in the palm of her hand. It provides a tactile reminder to the rider that she must close her fingers around the ball or risk dropping it—and when she does, I make her get off and pick it up herself. Pretty quickly, riders start to hold both the ball and their reins more correctly (fig. 9.22 A)! This may sound funny, but the best option I have found for *Fingers-Closed Balls* are commercial cat toys. You can choose foam ones or fuzzy ones, but they must be soft or else the rider won't be able to develop the correct "soft but firm" feel she is looking for in the hand on a rein. Cat toys are affordable, accessible, and won't scare or injure a horse if they are dropped or stepped on (fig. 9.22 B).

As with all of our Training Tools, the *Fingers-Closed Balls* should not become a crutch. Ride with them for a portion of your session, then set them aside and see if you can maintain the correction.

A

B

9.22 A & B The *Fingers-Closed Balls* help to train the rider to keep her fingers closed securely around the reins (A). I like regular cat toys for the *Fingers-Closed Balls* (B). They are soft to hold and are inexpensive to replace if you lose one.

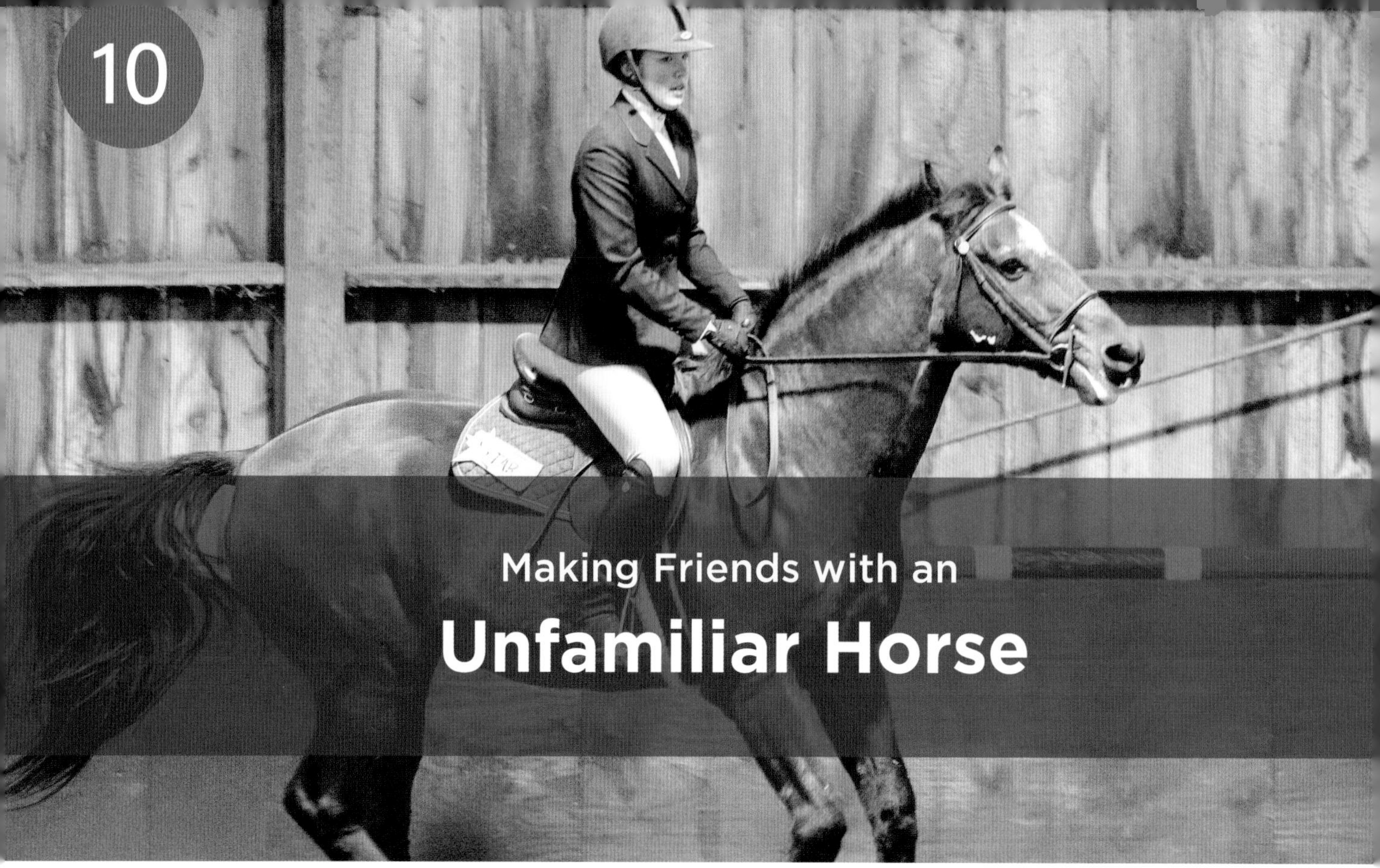

10

Making Friends with an Unfamiliar Horse

Most riders enjoy special bonds with different animals throughout the course of their equestrian careers. Each individual horse brings his own unique strengths to the arena, and savvy instructors strategically partner students with the best horse to challenge skills and encourage growth. As a rider's balance, control of the aids, and understanding of riding theory all become more sophisticated, the variety of different types of horse she can safely manage widens.

Every horse has something to teach us, and when a rider tries new horses, she is guaranteed to learn more about how horses think, act, and react to different situations. Ultimately, riding different horses makes her a better rider-athlete. Throughout my nearly five decades in the saddle, I have ridden hundreds of different horses of all shapes and sizes, at all levels of training, and in many different disciplines. Each one has taught me something different.

Throughout her career, a rider is likely to be offered many unique opportunities to sit on horses other than her own. Whether it is a chance to go foxhunting in Ireland, try a new sport like Polocrosse, experience the thrill of cantering through the Atlantic surf, or simply share a trail ride with a friend, a rider should always feel she has enough confidence in her skills that she can enthusiastically accept any invitation to ride (figs. 10.1 and 10.2).

Unfortunately, if a rider has had only limited opportunities to ride different types of horses, she may feel unprepared to try riding a

10.1 A rider should feel she has enough confidence to try riding a horse under any circumstances. Here Emmaree gets to ride on the beach.

new horse, especially under unfamiliar circumstances. The good news is that the fundamental skills and strengthening exercises you have been practicing throughout this book will give you a solid base upon which to build a new skill set: how to make friends with an unfamiliar horse.

This chapter is divided into two sections. In the first half, I discuss the process of trying out an unfamiliar horse that you might be considering for lease or purchase, focusing primarily on initial interactions, assessment of his under-saddle work, and your first ride. In the second half, I will address the specific challenges faced by scholastic/collegiate competition riders, who must successfully create and execute a plan to safely and confidently compete on a horse wholly unfamiliar to them.

10.2 Trying new horses and new sports improves us as riders. Amelie tries out the sport of polocrosse.

At first a rider should practice evaluating unfamiliar horses with the help of her trainer. Not only does the trainer know her students' strengths and weaknesses, she often can also predict how her student will interact with a given animal. With practice, all riders can train their eye to notice certain important clues about a new horse's attitude and behavior. However, if you see something in a horse's way of going, manners, or behavior that makes you feel uncertain and no qualified professional help is available, declining the ride is always your safest choice.

TRYING A HORSE FOR LEASE OR PURCHASE

"Test riding" a horse for lease or purchase is perhaps one of the most common situations in which a rider must work with an unfamiliar mount. Whenever possible, observe someone else riding the new horse first. Ideally, watch him work with his trainer, one of her students, and your own trainer before you get on yourself. Horses can and do behave differently, depending on who is in the saddle!

I base my initial assessment of the horse on

10.3 Take note of the bit used on a horse you are trying for the first time. A snaffle bit can indicate that the horse has a soft mouth and is responsive to the rider's hand.

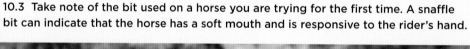

three main areas: the equipment that he and his rider use, his attitude or demeanor, and his responsiveness to the aids.

Equipment Check

The equipment chosen for a horse by the trainer or rider can give you some clues as to his attitude, behavior, or performance. As with many aspects of horsemanship, there are exceptions to every rule, but in my experience the equipment chosen is informative.

In general, a horse with a snaffle bit is going to have a softer mouth and be more responsive to the rider's hand than a horse wearing a pelham (fig. 10.3). Horses that require leverage bits, including pelhams, kimberwickes, gags, or three-ring "bubble bits," often earn this equipment because they lean on the rider's hand or require a stronger rein aid to get rebalanced, particularly over fences (fig. 10.4).

10.4 A leverage bit can indicate that the horse needs a stronger rein aid to stay balanced. The rider will need to stay deep in her leg and strong in her core to prevent her body from being pulled forward.

When I see a horse wearing a leverage bit, I know that the rider will need to stay deep in her leg and strong in her core to prevent her body from being pulled forward. In general, the stronger the bit in the mouth, the softer the rider's hand must be. Of course, the rider should still be tactful with her hands even when the horse is wearing a simple eggbutt snaffle! I hope by now you have practiced the exercises in this book enough to allow for the correct use of the elbow, without tension, and you have learned to be a tactful, soft rider, skills that will serve you well no matter what the horse wears in his mouth.

Occasionally, certain styles of leverage bits become trendy within a given discipline. If I notice many horses in a trainer's barn wearing the same style of strong bit, I make a mental note that a milder bit may be preferred if we end up taking the horse home.

When the rider is carrying a crop, wearing spurs, or both, it is easy to assume that the horse she is riding is not highly reactive to the leg aid. But in some disciplines, most riders use both types of artificial aids on all horses. For example, when an event rider is on cross-country, it

ARTIFICIAL AIDS

10.5 A & B **Maluihi rides with a crop (A), which is a sturdy, short tool used by jumping riders, and a whip (B), longer and more flexible than a crop, and used mostly in dressage.**

Artificial aids should always be used to supplement (not replace) the rider's natural aids (leg, seat, hands, voice, and eyes). The most common artificial aids are the crop or dressage whip, spurs, and martingales. When correctly used, artificial aids can significantly enhance the horse's responsiveness to the rider without needing to resort to extreme force or other abusive practices. But when used incorrectly, artificial aids magnify the rider's effect until the horse has no choices other than to shut down completely or act out in defiance.

Many variables affect the need for artificial aids. For example, due to their breed or temperament, some horses are inherently sluggish and can be more easily motivated with the support of a crop or spur. Others have a naturally high head carriage, and the gentle reminder of a martingale encourages lowering of the neck. At higher levels of training, the spur elicits a more refined response to the rider's leg, sharpening the horse's answer without causing him pain or distress.

Crops and whips are used to support the rider's leg aid. Sometimes the terms "crop" and "whip" are used interchangeably, but these are distinct pieces of equipment used in specific situations. A crop refers to the sturdy, short tool used by jumping riders in both hunt seat and eventing. For equitation classes, the shorter the crop, the better, and it should always be completely black, as we want our aids (artificial or natural) to be nearly invisible (fig. 10.5 A). A whip is much longer and more flexible than a crop; it is used most often in dressage (fig. 10.5 B).

Spurs refine the rider's leg aid, resulting in a more efficient response. They come in many different shapes, lengths, and styles, and a rider should work with her coach to choose the best spur for a specific horse. In general, always start with the smallest spur possible, going to a longer-necked spur only if the response is insufficient. Spurs should only be worn by riders who have learned to keep their leg quiet and still against the horse's side.

Martingales are useful for horses that naturally carry their heads too high. The martingale applies pressure when the horse lifts his head and neck above a certain threshold, releasing immediately when the head and neck are lowered. There are several styles of martingale, but the most common are the *standing* and *running* varieties.

Standing martingales are quite common when schooling or showing hunters over fences. They attach to a cavesson noseband, and when the horse lifts his head too high, he will feel

10.6 A & B The standing martingale attaches to the girth and cavesson noseband to help keep the horse's head down (A). The running martingale allows the horse more freedom in the neck than a standing martingale (B). It is most commonly seen in jumpers or eventers.

pressure on the bridge of his nose until he lowers his head again (fig. 10.6 A).

A *running* martingale allows the horse more freedom in his head and neck than does a standing martingale and is more commonly seen in the jumper arena or in eventing. Running martingales split into a left and a right branch, with each branch linked to a ring that slides over the corresponding rein (fig. 10.6 B). When the martingale is in effect, the horse feels pressure on the bars of his mouth through the reins. Running martingales require the rider to have educated hands because if she lifts them too high, she can inadvertently place a great deal of torque on the horse's mouth. The reins should be threaded through the martingale rings just before mounting; when leading a horse in a running martingale, the branches should be disconnected from the reins and looped around the neckpiece.

There are other artificial aids—draw reins, German martingales, chambons, and more—but most of these are training aids only and not legal for use in competition. In general, I have always felt that the simpler, the better. By learning to ride properly, you will have little use for many of these devices.

10.7 Take note of the size, style, length, and severity of any spur being used.

is imperative that the horse answer her natural aids immediately, so riders use artificial aids to promptly reinforce a lackadaisical response.

Back when I trained young, crossbred horses to be sold as foxhunters, I always carried a dressage whip, because if the horse didn't understand my leg aid, I needed something strong enough to ensure that the horse would keep going forward. Therefore, even if the rider is carrying a crop and wearing spurs, it is smart to still treat the horse as if he is quite sensitive to the leg, at least at first. You can always add more leg pressure, but it is hard to take it back when you "goose" a sensitive horse!

If the rider is wearing spurs, notice the style, length, size, and severity. Be sure to take into account the height of the rider versus the size of the horse when determining the horse's reactivity to the spur. For example, a tall, long-legged rider on a pony or narrow-sided horse may require a longer-necked spur in order to touch the horse's side, as her heel is likely well below the horse's barrel; in this case, the longer neck does not make the effect of the spur increase (fig. 10.7).

Noticing that a skilled rider is *not* using certain artificial aids is also informative. When the horse appears sluggish or lazy, yet the rider does not carry a crop or wear spurs, this can be a red flag as it often means that the horse is overreactive to one or both of these artificial aids. If a horse cannot tolerate a crop, it tells me his trainer hasn't done a full job of exposing the horse to every situation. There are some exceptions—for example, horses that have suffered mistreatment, or highly sensitive animals such as some off-track Thoroughbreds. But many times, if the horse is lazy and the rider does not carry a crop, it is because he overreacts to its use by running through the rider's hand or even by kicking out or bucking.

Attitude and Demeanor

How a horse acts under saddle is influenced by his temperament and his attitude. *Temperament* is constant and genetically driven, whereas *attitude* is variable and influenced by the situation. This is why one horse may react differently to a stimulus than a stablemate in the same training program.

As the horse warms up, pay attention to his body language. Does his eye remain calm and his posture relaxed? How does he carry his body with the rider on board? Are his ears mostly quiet, moving in response to the rider's aids? If the rider asks the horse to halt, does he stand patiently, or is he fidgeting and distracted? Watch his tail as he moves; a relaxed horse's tail will swing softly side to side. Overall, does the horse seem willing to be ridden?

Horses are usually at their best when they are working in a space and performing an activity with which they are familiar. It is quite common for a horse's attitude to change when moving from an indoor arena to the outdoor, or from the outdoor to an open field or trail. Some horses act differently while flatting than they do over fences. For the most accurate assessment, try to observe the horse performing under the conditions in which you expect to ride him yourself.

Reaction to the Rider's Aids

Finally, I assess how the horse reacts to the rider's hand, seat, upper body position, and leg aids.

When the rider applies pressure on the reins, does the horse respond with tension—such as becoming inverted in his neck or yanking the reins away—or does he softly yield, calmly chewing the bit and flexing his neck?

How does the rider manage the horse's transitions? Does she start out with a squeeze at first, only going to a stronger aid when the horse ignores the softer one? Or does the horse require a squeeze and five kicks and a tap of the crop to make the transition happen?

The upward transition to canter is especially telling. If the rider lifts her inside rein in an exaggerated fashion, or overbends the horse to the inside, these are good clues that

CATCH RIDES

To simplify the language in this section, I refer to competitions as "collegiate shows," but the information applies to any show held in a "catch ride" format. Always study the rulebook of the hosting organization for guidelines regarding horse selection, tack adjustment, and safety protocols.

it may be difficult for the horse to pick up his inside lead.

When the rider keeps her upper body extremely upright or even gets a little behind the motion, she may be anticipating a buck. When the rider stays in a light seat or two-point position in the canter, this can be a sign that the horse is tight in the back. These "cold-backed" horses can be inclined to buck when a rider sits too heavily or uses her seat too actively, which is important information to know before getting on board.

GETTING ACQUAINTED UNDER SADDLE

Horses appreciate a rider who is confident, clear with her aids, and willing to praise him efficiently for a correct response. Not all horses and riders are compatible with each other; in fact, it is often a case of "opposites attract." Sensitive horses tend to do well with calm, non-reactive riders, while high-strung or anxious riders are best suited to a quieter, more mellow mount.

If you and your coach have determined

COACH SALLY'S GUIDE TO EQUINE ETIQUETTE: SAYING HELLO

A horse lover sometimes can't contain her excitement when she is greeting a horse, particularly if the horse is one with whom she hopes to bond. But a good horseman always remembers that the horse quite literally does not see the world in the same way humans do, and this knowledge must affect how we approach and handle him.

As the horse evolved from a fox-sized creature into the *Equus caballus* of today, he developed many adaptations to enable him to survive life in his home on the open prairie or tundra. Because horses are a prey species that spend the majority of their day grazing with their heads lowered, they have nearly 360-degree vision and the reflex to move quickly away from any sudden movement (fig. 10.8). These

10.8 Due to their monocular vision, horses can see nearly 360 degrees around their body. This adaptation was essential for species survival.

that the unfamiliar horse seems safe and within your capabilities to ride, then the real fun can start! But don't let excitement interfere with your ability to approach the process of getting to know him under saddle in a thoughtful, methodical manner.

Ideally, ride the horse in the same arena in which the warm-up rider demonstrated his skills to you. Even if the horse warmed up with open gates in the ring, ask to close them before you put your own foot in the stirrup.

When I tried potential school horses for our collegiate program, if I ran into trouble, it was usually within the first few minutes of the ride. As a result, I insist that any unfamiliar horse is held by a competent handler at the mounting block when the rider first climbs aboard (fig. 10.10).

Keep your crop or whip (if you have one) in your left hand and be sure to hold the reins with a light contact while mounting, even though someone is holding the horse. This should be

qualities ensured the horse's survival because he could be on the run long before any predator launched an attack. Today, domesticated horses retain these wild traits.

With eyes on the sides of his head, the horse sees a different field of vision with his right eye versus his left; scientists call this *monocular vision*. The horse can see quite well around most of his body but has limited vision directly in front or behind. These are called *blind spots*. By contrast, humans (and other predatory species, such as cats and dogs) have eyes on the front of the head, with a widely overlapping field of vision. This is called *binocular vision*, and it gives us better depth perception and acuity than the horse.

Inexperienced equestrians often approach the horse by reaching out to pet him on the forehead. Doing this is extremely poor manners and will not make a good first impression! Due to the horse's blind spot directly in front of him, it is as if the hand appears out of nowhere, and most horses will lift their head in surprise.

Instead, approach a horse from his side, and first reach toward him lower on his body, around the shoulder or chin (fig. 10.9). This helps to start your new relationship on a harmonious note.

10.9 Morgan approaches Rayelle's horse from his side instead of reaching to pet him from in front.

10.10 When mounting an unfamiliar horse, it is a good idea to have a competent handler holding him.

your habit each and every time you mount, but a surprising number of riders seem to forget this important step. The handler should continue to hold the horse while you softly settle yourself into the saddle and make any necessary adjustments, then walk along with you for a few strides as you move away from the block.

Start at the walk and stay on a 20-meter circle. Run through a quick checklist of your position. Are your shoulders stacked over your hips? Are you maintaining a light, steady contact with about 5 pounds of pressure in each rein, while riding with a bent, elastic elbow? Is your leg stretched down and around the horse's barrel, securely in place without gripping? It is normal to be anxious on a new horse, but it is important to not allow that energy to be translated into tension in your body (fig. 10.11).

If everything is going well, add a quiet leg aid and increase it gradually until the horse transitions from walk to trot. Remain on the circle until you feel stable and balanced, then turn the circle into a figure eight. As you become more comfortable, try a canter.

At first, it is common that a rider will "miscue" a new horse, using too much leg when she needed only a little, or too little rein and seat in a downward transition when she needed a bit more. Don't be discouraged—this is all part of the challenge of being a horseman. Stay committed to the good habits you have practiced using the Athletic Equestrian system, and, before long, communication between you and your new mount will become clearer.

ASSESSING YOUR COLLEGIATE HORSE SHOW DRAW

For varsity riders, being able to get on an unfamiliar mount and produce a winning ride is an essential skill. At collegiate shows, horses are always warmed up in front of the competitors; careful evaluation of this warm-up phase is essential to creating an effective plan for your ride (fig. 10.12 A). In general, my assessment covers the same critical areas as when I try out a new horse—equipment check, attitude/demeanor, responsiveness to the aids—with a few additional considerations in each area (fig. 10.12 B).

At most collegiate competitions, riders entered in the show are not allowed to warm up horses. Show managers frequently rely on other riders from the host barn to perform this essential duty, some of whom may not be as

10.11 When trying a new horse, try to stay as relaxed as possible. If you find yourself getting nervous, just stop, give the horse a knuckle rub, and smile like Evy is doing here.

10.12 A & B At collegiate competitions, the horses are warmed up in front of the exhibitors (A). This is your time to watch and observe how the horses behave. Suehayla and Sophia watch the horses warm up to gain insight into what each horse needs (B).

experienced as the competitors. If a horse looks challenging to ride during the warm-up, I evaluate the skills of his rider. If she appears to be less experienced, it is possible that a more experienced rider, using normal aids with better timing, will establish a more positive result. If a warm-up rider appears to be having a significant negative impact on a horse's performance, I will ask a steward to see if the horse can be schooled by someone else.

Equipment Check

At collegiate horse shows, horse providers or show hosts determine which horses may be ridden with a crop and/or with spurs and ensure that these animals are warmed up accordingly. Athletes and coaches are not allowed to simply decide that a certain horse should be ridden with a crop or spur, even if he appears to be quite lazy. Remember, the horse provider or show host is the one who knows the horse best, and she wants to ensure that each horse has the opportunity to do his job happily and successfully (fig. 10.13).

HORSE DESCRIPTIONS

MUDDY BROOK

Dan: 16.3h Dark Bay, TB Gelding, Ride him soft in your hand, huge stride, balance in the corners, does have changes, fun draw!

Dolly: 16.1h Gray Mare. Crop optional. Balance in the corners support with leg. Pretty straight forward. Can get on the forehand, keep balanced in corners. Will do changes if you ask.

Gambit: 16h Bay Gelding, crop optional, can be lazy keep leg on, prefers soft light contact on the flat, simple changes.

J.T.: 16.1h Flea Bitten Gray Gelding, crop optional, Ride with a soft hand, keep inside leg on to help hold out in turns, simple changes.

OAK HILL FARM

Diamond: 16 h grey th gelding. Has lead change. Soft hands and seat. Rides like a hunter.

Tigger: 16.3 h warmblood grey gelding. Has a lead change. Don't let him get behind your leg and package him. Nice draw, good soul.

Winston: 15 h gelding bay, can anticipate. Keep on rail. Let him do his job, ask for lead. Good draw.

Goodie: 15.2 h chestnut gelding. Been there, done that. Soft hands and seat. Good guy, simple change.

Bruce: 14.2 h Connemara bay gelding. Hunter. Has lead change. Spurs always. Soft hands. Runs on candy.

DARTMOUTH COLLEGE

Brady: 16 h big, beautiful, and blonde. Loves watching romantic comedies. Simple change. Use outside aids for turns.

Garth: 17h bay gelding. Lazy, keep your leg on, be soft in hand. He just wants to drink his coffee in his rocking chair on the front porch in peace.

Bodie: 15.1 h QH gelding. Straight forward. Soft hand. Steady-eddie of our school horse string. As our shortest school horse, Bodie likes to say he's "small but mighty"! Weight limit: 160 pounds Height limit: 5'10"

Beamer: 18 hands of tall, chestnut, and handsome. Ride like a hunter, stay soft, do not curl up into a frame. Flying change.

Dutch: 17 h Dutch Warmblood. Soft hand. Flying change. Leased to us by a nearby barn. Dutch is still in touch with his friends at his old barn and sends them daily snapchats.

Slick: 17.2 h warmblood gelding. Slick is a solid boy and brags that he can bench press more than any varsity athlete, but has yet to show up in the Varsity gym to prove it.

10.13 At collegiate competitions, only the horse providers can decide if the horse needs a spur or crop. Here is a sample horse description sheet with the Dartmouth team adding in some humor.

Even if a warm-up rider carries a crop or wears spurs, don't assume that you must do so as well. If you have only limited experience using a crop or spurs at home, then using either of these tools on a new horse is probably not a recipe for success. Additionally, I consider the rider's conformation before allowing her to use spurs. For example, a rider who is 4 foot 11 inches on a broad, big-barreled horse will end up using the spur higher on his body than he is accustomed to, possibly resulting in a much greater reaction to the aid. In collegiate competition, I always preferred the possibility that a rider would not be able to motivate her horse to go forward over creating a situation that was potentially unsafe.

Attitude/Demeanor

It is not your job to train the horse to get over his issues during your collegiate show ride. However, if your draw is a lesson horse, practicing a little "equine psychology" may help to get the best performance from him.

Many lesson horses are a bit herdbound, and they express this in several ways. The horse may bulge his outside shoulder toward the gate each time he passes it or be reluctant to start on course while his friends remain outside the ring. Other horses drift toward their friends in the arena or are reluctant to leave the rail and pass a slower horse. Some spiral gradually toward the middle of the ring, until they are making a tiny circle in the center instead of a full lap of the outside edge.

If the horse bulges toward the gate or seems reluctant to pass other horses, the rider should carry her crop and extra reins (the "bight") to the outside (fig. 10.14). When she rides past the gate or leaves the rail, she gives the horse a reminder tap on his shoulder with the crop. If the horse drifts toward the middle, riders should carry the crop against the inside shoulder, giving tactful reminders with it if the horse loses his track.

Some horses do not care to be crowded and respond quite strongly when other horses get too close. If the horse puts his ears back, grinds his teeth, or kicks out when other horses pass by, or if he wears a red ribbon in his tail (which

10.14 When a horse bulges toward the gate, the rider should carry her crop and extra reins to the outside.

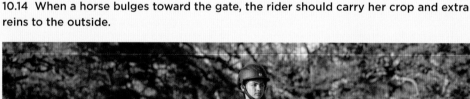

warns riders that the horse may kick), it will be critical to keep this horse away from others in the arena (fig. 10.15). Even if you do not draw this horse yourself, be aware of his position in the ring and try to keep your distance. A great way to practice this skill at home is to ride in group lessons, where each rider must practice maintaining her own spacing throughout the schooling session.

Collegiate shows have a way of bringing out even the calmest lesson horse's sassy side. With riders, coaches, spectators, and lots of nervous energy crowding into a normally quiet arena, horses may be spooky or distracted at first. Fortunately, most horses relax as the warm-up goes along.

If your draw still seems unsettled before your ride, try to identify the specific stimulus upsetting him. If he seems to be spooking only at one end of the arena, then plan to turn early as you approach that area. If the horse is distracted by something outside of the arena, plan to gently turn his head away from the distraction, then ride forward.

It is always up to the rider and her coach to decide if the horse's behavior is something she can safely manage. Approach a show steward with any safety concerns.

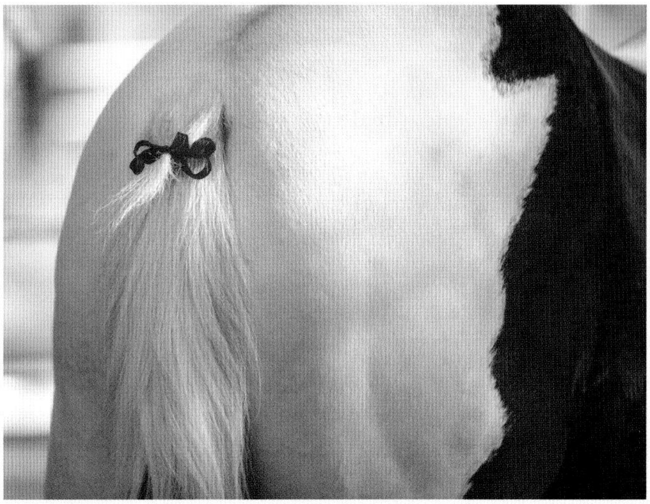

10.15 When a horse wears a red ribbon in his tail, it means that he might kick, so it is best to keep your distance.

Responsiveness to the Aids

As discussed in the previous section, carefully watch the mount's reaction to the warm-up rider's aids. Does he maintain each gait willingly, with only an occasional, gentle reminder from the rider's leg, or does he rely on the rider to actively cue him to keep moving? Does the horse demonstrate a clear, three-beat canter, or does he occasionally lose impulsion, fall onto his forehand, and move closer to a four-beat rhythm, or even drop into the trot?

In equitation, a break of gait is a significant fault, right up there with posting on the wrong diagonal, or picking up the incorrect lead, and it will put a rider to the bottom of the judge's card (fig. 10.16). If you draw this type of horse, you will need to be prepared to use assertive aids to maintain his energy in each gait. If flat classes run prior to yours, note where the judge is standing in the arena and where her focus stays. If it becomes necessary to use a larger aid such as a kick or even a tap of the crop, ideally this is done away from the judge's eye.

Pay close attention to how the warm-up

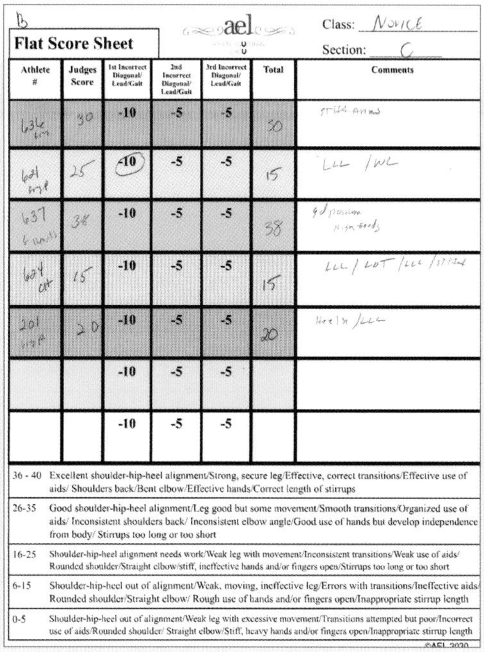

B

Flat Score Sheet

ael

Class: Novice

Section: C

Athlete #	Judges Score	1st Incorrect Diagonal/ Lead/Gait	2nd Incorrect Diagonal/ Lead/Gait	3rd Incorrect Diagonal/ Lead/Gait	Total	Comments
636	30	-10	-5	-5	30	stiff arms
621	25	-10	-5	-5	15	LLL / WL
637	38	-10	-5	-5	38	gd position high hands
624	15	-10	-5	-5	15	LLL / LOT / LLL / stiff
201	20	-10	-5	-5	20	Heels / LLL
		-10	-5	-5		
		-10	-5	-5		

36 - 40	Excellent shoulder-hip-heel alignment/Strong, secure leg/Effective, correct transitions/Effective use of aids/ Shoulders back/Bent elbow/Effective hands/Correct length of stirrups
26-35	Good shoulder-hip-heel alignment/Leg good but some movement/Smooth transitions/Organized use of aids/ Inconsistent shoulders back/ Inconsistent elbow angle/Good use of hands but develop independence from body/ Stirrups too long or too short
16-25	Shoulder-hip-heel alignment needs work/Weak leg with movement/Inconsistent transitions/Weak use of aids/ Rounded shoulder/Straight elbow/stiff, ineffective hands and/or fingers open/Stirrups too long or too short
6-15	Shoulder-hip-heel out of alignment/Weak, moving, ineffective leg/Errors with transitions/Ineffective aids/ Rounded shoulder/Straight elbow/ Rough use of hands and/or fingers open/Inappropriate stirrup length
0-5	Shoulder-hip-heel out of alignment/Weak leg with excessive movement/Transitions attempted but poor/Incorrect use of aids/Rounded shoulder/ Straight elbow/Stiff, heavy hands and/or fingers open/Inappropriate stirrup length

©AEL 2020

10.16 A break of gait, along with posting on the wrong diagonal, or cantering on the wrong lead, can move you down on a judge's scorecard. This Athletic Equestrian League flat scoresheet shows both the judge's score and comments. In the comments section, the judge has noted that the riders have various position faults such as stiff arms; "LLL," which stands for "loose lower leg"; "WL," which means "wrong lead"; high hands; stiff overall; and heels not down enough.

rider uses her aids during transitions and the horse's response to them. If the rider cues the horse to trot and he moves off as if shot from a cannon, look to see if the rider's leg is soft or if she has dug a spur into his side. By contrast, if the horse is reluctant to make the transition, what does the rider do next? Assuming that the warm-up rider has some knowledge of the horse's usual manners and way of going, her response to the horse's resistance gives you good clues as to the best way to manage him.

COACH SALLY'S TOP 10 TIPS

Tip 10: Respect Your Coach

The many instructors and coaches I have worked with throughout my own career have each helped to shape my personal riding style and philosophy. Listening to feedback from different coaches provides riders with new insights, perceptions and techniques for addressing issues in their riding (fig. 10.17 A). You never know when hearing a unique way of explaining a familiar concept will cause a "lightbulb moment" significant enough to drive an important correction home.

Even if the rider disagrees with the feedback she receives, it is important to show these professionals the respect they deserve. Whether she is riding with her regular coach, an assistant coach, or a guest instructor or clinician, a rider should never dismiss what a riding instructor says to her outright. Just as every horse has something to teach a rider, there is something to be learned from every coach or trainer a rider encounters throughout her career, so long as she keeps an open mind (fig. 10.17 B).

Experienced coaches understand that it can take time for new riders to adjust to their coaching style and expectations. They encourage riders to respectfully ask questions when necessary, but also to be observant of how other riders in the coach's program act and behave. When riders join a

10.17 A & B Riding with different coaches provides new insights. For spring break each year, I took my Dartmouth team to Ocala, Florida, to ride with Kim Burnette at Kimberden (A). Something can be learned from every coach that you ride with. Maluihi listens intently to her coach Tiare at Kawailoa Ranch in Haleiwa, Hawaii (B).

collegiate or varsity team, it is expected that they follow the coach's training system completely. Varsity athletes know that when they ride with their team coach, they are required to ride the way the coach teaches them to.

On occasion, there will be times when a lesson leaves the rider confused or in need of further clarification. When this happens, I encourage the rider to set up an appointment outside of her lesson to talk through the exercise or concept further. Don't take time away from other riders in your group or the next lesson by monopolizing your coach's attention, and certainly never argue with the coach or talk back.

At the end of every lesson, practice, or coaching session, thank your coach. Ask her for a takeaway to think about and practice for your next lesson. These simple habits show that you respect the coach and appreciate her time (fig. 10.18).

10.18 The Dartmouth College Varsity Equestrian Team celebrates a team victory at their home competition along with Intercollegiate Horse Shows Association Founder Bob Cacchione.

Conclusion

By practicing my Athletic Equestrian training system daily and making it part of your usual routine, you will become a more correctly aligned, athletic, fit, and balanced rider athlete. Further, you will be more in tune with your horse and better able to work with him as a partner.

To complement the Athletic Equestrian training system, many rider athletes also benefit from unmounted cross-training at least two or three times per week. This could include gym workouts, hiking, running, swimming, cycling, or any other activity that helps boost cardiovascular fitness. While I've yet to find an unmounted workout that targets all of the exact muscles needed for riding, I believe that Pilates comes closest. Pilates workouts

Following my Athletic Equestrian system can lead to great results. Cristiana wears the Dartmouth "Winner's Flair" flanked by Claire and Staci.

Teaching has taken me around the world, including Hawaii and South Africa. None of this would have happened if I hadn't been willing to reach beyond my comfort zone to see where horses could take me.

include both stretching and strength building, and emphasize key core exercises that lead to improved body control on the horse.

To conclude, I want to leave you with what has become my life motto: "Seize the opportunity." I encourage you to move forward in your equestrian career by taking advantage of every opportunity available to you with an open mind, because you quite literally never know where it might lead. Personally, I have traveled around the world—to Australia to research the sport of polocrosse and write the first-ever book on the subject, all over the United States (including Alaska and Hawaii) to teach clinics, and even to South Africa to work with enthusiastic students who had traveled from all over the country to meet me. None of this would have happened if I hadn't been willing to reach beyond my comfort zone to see where horses could take me.

Learn More!

Learn how to ride like a varsity athlete and book a clinic with Sally Batton! All ages and abilities will benefit from Sally's attentive and positive teaching style.

Contact Sally at athleticequestrian@gmail.com

Navigating the world of collegiate riding is a mystery to most young rider athletes and their families. Join podcast host Sally Batton as she interviews collegiate coaches, riders, and organizations for their insight on what it takes to ride on a collegiate equestrian team.

Athletic Equestrian Riding in College Podcast
Available on Apple Podcasts and Spotify

Coach Sally Batton with some of Dartmouth Equestrian's ribbons and trophies.

About the Authors

Sally Batton was the head coach of the Dartmouth College Division I Varsity Equestrian Team for 30 years, coaching dozens of riders to regional, zone, and national titles. Previously, she spent six years as assistant coach of the team at Centenary University (New Jersey), bringing both individuals and the team to national competition. She is the past Intercollegiate Horse Shows Association (IHSA) National Steward, and in 2013, she was presented with the IHSA Lifetime Achievement Award in recognition of her contributions and leadership within the organization. In 2020, Coach Batton was inducted into the inaugural class of the IHSA Hall of Fame.

An avid polocrosse enthusiast, Batton is a past board member of the American Polocrosse Association (APA), past member of the United States Pony Club Polocrosse Committee, a certified APA Polocrosse Coach, and the author of *Polocrosse: Australian Made, Internationally Played* (Belcris, 1990).

Batton is a certified instructor with both the United States Hunter Jumper Association (USHJA) and the American Riding Instructor's Association (ARIA); in 2008, she was named ARIA Instructor of the Year. She is the founder and president of the Athletic Equestrian League, an organization that offers horsemanship education and competition opportunities to English and Western riders from first grade through adult. She is also the host of the Athletic Equestrian Riding in College Podcast.

Batton holds an Equestrian Studies degree from Lake Erie College and a master's degree in Communications from Fairleigh-Dickinson University.

Christina Keim, M. Ed., M.F.A., is an award-winning narrative journalist with nearly 1,000 published articles to her credit. Her work has appeared in *The Chronicle of the Horse, UnTacked, Equine Journal, Practical Horseman, The Eastern Equerry, Northeast Equestrian Life, Green Mountain Horse Association Magazine, Woodstock Magazine,* and *The Plaid Horse,* among others. She is a senior lecturer in the Equine Studies Program at the University of New Hampshire, where she has also been the head coach of their Intercollegiate Horse Shows Association hunt seat team since 2004.

Acknowledgments

I must thank several key people both in my equestrian "family" and my actual family who have been critical to my progress and success in the horse world. I start with my profound appreciation to my co-author, colleague, and friend, Christina Keim. I knew I couldn't do this project alone and needed someone to take all my scattered ramblings and form them into coherent paragraphs, pages, and chapters. While I often moaned when she would ask me for more detail or a deeper description, it always led to exactly what I was trying to convey! Christina's ability to turn my thoughts and concepts into the written word constantly amazes me and I will forever be indebted to her patience, humor, and talents.

I also want to thank my colleague and friend, CJ Law, head coach of the Mount Holyoke College Equestrian Team in Massachusetts for over 35 years. Throughout my tenure at Dartmouth, I relied on CJ's expertise and deep knowledge of both the horse and his rider athlete to help me in my own quest to produce top riders. Her devotion to her athletes and their success is second to none and I hold the deepest admiration and respect for her. I also need to tip my riding hat to CJ for first introducing me to the idea of using Teaching Tools to bring out the best in our rider athletes. As coaches, we walk into the arena each day with our personal bag of Teaching Tools in our continual quest to produce the best, and I remain indebted to CJ for her personal contributions to my own "instructor's toolkit."

Thank you to my photographers Amanda Terbrusch, Ashley Yeaton, and Olivia Yossa. Special thanks to all the athletes who were my models for this book and to the six main facilities where the photos were taken: Koko Crater Stables, Honolulu, Hawaii; Maunawili Farms, Kailua, Hawaii; Kawailoa Ranch in Haleiwa, Hawaii; Over the Oxer in Dover, New Hampshire; Jamaica Bay Riding Academy in Brooklyn, New York; and Floyd Woods Farm in Chester, New Hampshire.

Thank you to Nancy Kohler-Cunningham, Lilli Bieler Biedermann, and Suzanne McGovern, who each devoted time and energy to reading drafts of this book with a critical eye for content and flow. Your suggestions

The Dartmouth Equestrian Team celebrates a team win.

helped hone focus and clarity, and your enthusiasm confirmed that the Athletic Equestrian training system will prove valuable to riders from many backgrounds.

Thanks to my partner Ed, whose love and support has allowed me to follow my dreams, as well as to my sisters Susan and Pam, and my chosen sisters Maja and Lori for their encouragement and love.

And finally, I must thank the hundreds of Dartmouth Equestrian athletes who, over several decades, made me a better teacher and coach through their boundless enthusiasm and love for both the horses and our sport!

Index

Page numbers in *italics* indicate illustrations.